As an Fhearann
From the Land

Edited by
Malcolm MacLean and Christopher Carrell

MAINSTREAM
PUBLISHING
Edinburgh
an LANNTAIR
Stornoway
Third Eye Centre
Glasgow
1986

As an Fhearann / From the Land

First published 1986 on the occasion of *As an Fhearann / From the Land,* an exhibition initiated and organised by An Lanntair Gallery, Stornoway, to mark the Centenary of the Crofting Act 1886

Bunnahabhain

The publishers gratefully acknowledge the financial assistance of Bunnahabhain, the 12 Year Old Single Malt Scotch Whisky, distilled on the Island of Islay, in the publication of this volume. Islay has had a long connection both with crofting and with whisky distilling.

The publishers also gratefully acknowledge the financial support of the Scottish Arts Council.

Chuidich an Comann Leabhraichean am foillsichear le cosgaisean an leabhair seo.

Compiled and edited by Malcolm MacLean (An Lanntair Gallery) and Christopher Carrell (Third Eye Centre)

Designed by Christopher Carrell in association with Malcolm MacLean

Published by Mainstream Publishing, Edinburgh; An Lanntair Gallery, Stornoway; and Third Eye Centre, Glasgow

Distributed by Mainstream Publishing, 7 Albany Street, Edinburgh EH1 3UG, Scotland. Tel: 031 557 2959

Printed by E.F. Peterson, 12 Laygate, South Shields, Tyne & Wear

Title page top: *Carsaig Bay, near Tayvallich,* c1880s

"A deserted crofting settlement in Argyll, photographed at the height of the land agitation. Few crofters involved in the agitation were unaware of the verse in Isaiah *that reads, 'Your country is desolate, your cities are burned with fire; your land, strangers devour it in your presence, and it is desolate, as overthrown by strangers.'"*   Iain Fraser Grigor

Title page bottom: Robert Adam (1885-1967) *Tarskavaig, Isle of Skye, 24th September 1931.* Collection of *Scots Magazine*

As an Fhearann / From the Land
(As un Erun)

Cha robh glaodh a bha aig an t-siamarlan Dòmhnall Munro a chuireadh barrachd feagail air na daoine na: Cuiridh mi as an fhearann thu. Bho'n uairsin thug iad cuid mhath dé am beòshlainte agus an saothair as an fhearann. Ach an diugh, chan eil coltas nach eil ar dòighean a' gluasad nas fhaide 's nas fhaide as an fhearann. Ach càil a nì sinn mar shluagh — ann an dòigh, 's ann as an fhearann a tha e a' tighinn.

The crofter's pattern of living is geared intimately to the land from which his culture draws much of its colour and emphasis. In the past this phrase was also a common threat by the landowner's agent that the people would be "removed from the land" — "as an fhearann".

An Lanntair

Tha An Lanntair na lobhta neo-eisimeileach le taic bho Comhairle Ealdhain na h-Alba agus Comhairle nan Eilean. Dh'fhosgail An Lanntair anns a' Mhàrt 1985 agus 'se a' chiad lobhta ealdhain anns na h-Eileanan an lar.

An Lanntair is an independent gallery with charitable status supported by the Scottish Arts Council and the Western Isles Islands Council. An Lanntair opened in March 1985 and is the first art gallery in the Western Isles. An Lanntair translates as "The Lantern", and also as an arable or wooded area of land overlooking the sea.

Exhibition Tour Venues

An Lanntair *Stornoway*	26th July — 29th September 1986
Royal Scottish Museum *Edinburgh*	October 1986
Third Eye Centre *Glasgow*	8th November — 29th November 1986
Artspace *Aberdeen*	14th February — 4th March 1987
Inverness Art Gallery and Eden Court Theatre *Inverness*	March — April 1987
Crawford Centre for the Arts *St Andrews*	24th April— 24th May 1987

Below: Edwin Landseer (1803-1873) *Rent Day in the Wilderness.* Oil on canvas, 48" × 104", 1868. Collection of the National Galleries of Scotland

After the Jacobite defeat of 1715, Donald Murchison defended the confiscated Ross-shire estates of the attainted Earl of Seaforth and regularly transmitted rent to the exiled earl. Landseer pictured him here with the Seaforth rent book open in front of him.

Acknowledgements

The exhibition on which this book is based has been a major undertaking for a small gallery such as An Lanntair. Given the scale of the challenge, and An Lanntair's limited resources, it is inevitably incomplete. Apologies, for example, are due to our cousins elsewhere throughout the Highlands and Islands for our perspective being quite so clearly a view from the Western Isles. More general apologies are also offered in advance for any major omissions of imagery, information or acknowledgement which have been unobtainable or overlooked due to pressure of time.

It would be impossible to acknowledge everyone individually but sincere thanks are due to all who have assisted in the making of *As an Fhearann*. Neither the exhibition nor the book would have been possible without the goodwill and enthusiasm of many people who have given freely and generously of their time, energy and experience.

Particular thanks must go to Robby Neish, whose constant hard work, good humour and sense of order have held the multiplying elements of book and exhibition together throughout the past six months. Joni Buchanan has organised a major part of *As an Fhearann* as well as providing much of the historical information and coping calmly and expertly with impossible deadlines and expectations. Roddy Murray and Ros Paterson have given constant and generous assistance to each of *As an Fhearann*'s many parts, while Chrissie MacMillan, Catherine Smith and Annie Maynard patiently and expertly tackled the endless typing. Dolina MacKenzie provided numerous and speedy translations. Thanks are also due to Ian MacDonald, whose incisive eye and last minute guidance were invaluable.

The research was generously assisted by Iain Fraser Grigor, Jim Hunter, Bill Findlay, Ray Burnett, Colin MacArthur, Stuart Macdonald, Keith Hartley, Lindsay Errington, Gavin Sprott, Murdo John MacLeod, Cyril Gerber, John Prebble, the School of Scottish Studies, John MacInnes, Ann Matheson, Museum nan Eilean and Art Galleries throughout Scotland.

The support of Norman Buchan, Ian Noble, Brian Wilson, Kenneth Alexander, Ronald Cramond, Lindsay Gordon and especially Daniel Shackleton is gratefully acknowledged, as is the much appreciated co-operation of the Lewis Museum Society, Thompson, Craig & Donald, Acair Publishing, Peacock Printmakers, Image Machine, and George Oliver.

The effective professional advice of Robert Breen and Maggie Bolt and the commitment and expertise of Jane Carroll and Alasdair MacCallum of Central Designs enabled the 'idea' to be translated into the exhibition. Various artists and all of the writers represented here have made important contributions to the concept and structure of *As an Fhearann*, extending well beyond that which is obvious.

A special thankyou is due to Barbara and Murray Grigor for their hospitality and encouragement as well as unlimited access to their delightful Scotch Myths Archive. The same is due to Simon MacKenzie whose knowledge of the *Gaidhealtachd* and creative energy have so generously been made available for the benefit of both exhibition and book. I owe special thanks to various friends for different kinds of inspiration along the way and to my teaching colleagues for their forbearance.

My own contribution to exhibition and book is dedicated to the late Nellie Morrison and to my family.

Last but by no means least I would like to express particular gratitude to Frank Thompson, Sam Maynard and Chris Carrell whose various professional skills have wrought coherence out of apparent chaos and enabled this book to come into being.

Above: George Washington Wilson (1823-1893) *Crofter's House, Benbecula,* 1880s. Collection of L.M.H. Smith

Mitchell Library; National Library of Scotland; National Museums of Scotland; People's Palace Museum; *Punch* Magazine; Queen's Own Highlanders; School of Scottish Studies (Edinburgh University); Scotch Myths Archive; *Scots Magazine* (Robert Adam Collection); Scottish Arts Council Collection; Scottish National Gallery of Modern Art; Scottish National Portrait Gallery; Scottish Photography Group (Stills Gallery); Scottish Records Office; Scottish Tourist Authority; Seaforth Maritime; 7:84 Scotland; Spectrum Colour Library; Paul Strand Archive; Tate Gallery; Robert Allison; Ewan Bain; Manfred Bluth; Mr Campbell; Maxwell Deans; Robert Fleming Holdings; Iain Fraser Grigor; Mr G. Harrison; Norman Johnstone; Deirdre MacDonald; George MacDonald; Hamish MacLaren; Simon MacKenzie; Domhnull Mac'illeathain; Mrs James MacLean; Sorley MacLean; Peter MacLeod; Timothy Neat; George and Cordelia Oliver; Jack Shea; L.M.H. Smith; Mrs F. Sutherland; Daniel Shackleton; *The Stornoway Gazette*

As an Fhearann has been financially supported by . . .
The Scottish Arts Council
The Highlands and Islands Development Board
The Gulbenkian Foundation
Third Eye Centre
The Manpower Services Commission
Comhairle nan Eilean

Bunnahabhain Scotch Whisky
The West Highland Free Press
Western Isles Salmon
William Burns Engineering
K. MacKay and Co.
British Petroleum
British Telecom
Hebridean Yachts
The Harris Tweed Association
A.R. Davidson

The Gaelic Books Council
The Stornoway Trust
The Educational Institute of Scotland
The National Association of Local Govt. Officers (Western Isles)
The Scottish Trades Union Congress
Highland Heritage

The Editors would like to acknowledge their debt to Joni Buchanan for compiling the Chronology, the Bibliography and much of the picture text, and to those authors from whom they have quoted extensively throughout *As an Fhearann*: the work of James Hunter, Iain Fraser Grigor's *Mightier than a Lord* and *The Companion to Gaelic Scotland* (ed. Professor Derick S. Thomson) were particularly valuable.

An Lanntair gratefully acknowledges the loan of works, both for the exhibition and for reproduction in this book, from the following public and private collections:

Aberdeen Art Gallery; British Film Institute; John Dewar and Sons; Illustrated London News Picture Library; Kirkcaldy Art Gallery and Museum; Glasgow Art Galleries and Museums;

Malcolm MacLean
Organiser, *As an Fhearann*

Contents

NB A number of the paintings referred to by Alexander Moffat in his essay "Beyond the Highland Landscape" can be found in the Colour section, and in black and white elsewhere in the book. All text in italics, accompanying illustrations, compiled by the editors in association with Joni Buchanan.

Below: Gus Wylie *Snow and Sheep, Harris,* 1970s

Above: *Eviction of tenant farmers.* Engraving from Donald Ross *Real Scottish Grievances,* Glasgow 1854

"*Shifting of rural populations occurred throughout Europe as a result of changes in land use; what distinguished the Highland experience was that it occurred relatively late and was both sweeping and brutal because the Highland landlord possessed powers more unrestricted than those of any other in Europe*". Professor Derick S. Thomson (ed): *The Companion to Gaelic Scotland,* Oxford 1983

"*The cruellest and most important fact of all is that the criterion for the best use of land ceased to be the number of people it could support, and became the amount of profit it could make.*" John McGrath, 1986

"*We have to remember that many outsiders even today do not know what is meant by crofting. They do not know it is not just small scale farming, but a whole unique way of life from which the financial rewards are not necessarily the most important. Is it not a matter of great joy to recall that in their best years the crofters of Lewis reclaimed some two and a half thousand acres of some of the worst land in Great Britain when land improvement by surface reseeding was in its infancy elsewhere?*" Archie Gillespie, opening the Barvas Show, 1983

"*Land is the basic resource of the Highlands and Islands, and its private ownership overall by absentee landlords is an affront to economic development. Until such time as the present sterilisation of the land is tackled effectively, neither economic nor social progress can come to the area. A survey of land use was undertaken in 1969-70 but on the condition that the findings would be confidential. This is surely absurd in any democracy.*" The Companion to Gaelic Scotland, 1983

"*Wilderness is no longer a negative term*" — Countess of Sutherland, at a press conference held at the Ritz Hotel, London, to announce a scheme which would transform Dunrobin Castle into a luxury tourism complex. The developers are seeking £3.5 million of public money. West Highland Free Press, 19th February 1985

The Exiles

The many ships that left our country
with white wings for Canada.
They are like handkerchiefs in our memories
and the brine like tears
and in their masts sailors singing
like birds on branches.
That sea of May running in such blue,
a moon at night, a sun at daytime,
and the moon like a yellow fruit,
like a plate on a wall
to which they raise their hands
like a silver magnet
with piercing rays
streaming into the heart.

Iain Crichton Smith

Translated from the author's own Gaelic from *The Exiles,* Manchester 1984

As an Fhearann

As an Fhearann commemorates the 1886 Crofting Act. For those who are unaware of the history of the Highlands it may be something of a mystery as to why Highlanders attribute such significance to this event. For some, the ill-fated Jacobite rising of 1745, and its climax on Culloden Moor, might be thought more seminal. Culloden, however, was only the beginning of the cycle of events that were to desolate the Highlands and become known as "fuadach nan Gaidheal" or the "Highland Clearances".

The brutal aftermath of Culloden destroyed the old clan-system, while the rise of the Industrial Revolution heralded a new socio-economic order. The increasingly profligate and Anglicised clan chiefs came to see large sheep farms, and later deer parks, as more profitable than the traditional concept of 'clan lands' and the traditional patterns of land use. Families who had worked their land for generations came to be seen as an unprofitable liability. Throughout the North the land-owners, their factors, and their agents ruthlessly implemented policies of 'improvement'. A century of Highland history is dominated by population clearance, forced evictions, and emigration under duress.

The fertile inland straths and glens were given over to the sheep and the deer while the people were crowded onto emigrant ships or into the slums of swelling lowland cities. Those who remained were forced into congested pockets around the coast and left clinging to marginal lands with inferior soil next to the sea. They had absolutely no security of tenure and, despite famine and destitution, were forbidden to take even seaweed from the shorelands for use as fertiliser.

The extreme tensions generated by the land-issue culminated in major civil unrest, and a series of bitter confrontations between the dispossessed people and the land-owning interests. By the mid-1880s the civil unrest

Above: Sir Henry Raeburn (1756-1823) *Colonel Alastair Macdonell of Glengarry.* Oil on canvas, 95" × 59", c1812. Collection of the National Galleries of Scotland

Below: *An evicted Highland family amid the ruins of their croft,* c1880s. Collection of the Scottish Agricultural Museum

had prompted military intervention and the Napier Commission, which took evidence throughout the Highlands and Islands. The Commission's Report to the Government of the day resulted in the Crofting Act of 1886, which granted crofters hereditary security of tenure, established "fair and reasonable" rents, and fixed the average croft size.

The significance of the 1886 Crofting Act for the Highlands and Islands is, therefore, difficult to exaggerate. It not only halted the Clearances but represents a watershed which has shaped the subsequent history of the land and its people. The Crofting Act legislation continues to shape the pattern of life in the Highlands to this day.

An Lanntair was faced with the challenge of commemorating the centenary of the Act within a few months of opening in 1985. Situated in a Gaelic-speaking crofting community we were particularly aware of its importance. We were also aware of its imperfections, and that a complex of overlapping contemporary issues are involved if a commemoration is to be of more than solely historical interest. It is beyond the scope of any one exhibition to do full justice to these issues but they form some of the background to *As an Fhearann*.

The Act itself, for example, was a remarkable achievement but it did not restore the lost lands or resolve the Highland land question. That is an issue which continues to fester on quietly into the late twentieth century, erupting at irregular intervals into the public consciousness. Politically and economically the Highlands, and especially the Islands, are remote from the centres of power and continue to occupy a marginal and somewhat neglected position, similar to other peripheral regions and minority cultures worldwide. The crofting system which stemmed from the Act has provided the social fabric, and a hard-wrought material stability, for the Gael, but the gradual erosion of the Gaelic language and culture continues. These material and cultural issues are further complicated by the commercial success of recently invented traditions, from Balmorality to Brigadoon, which have tended to further distort and obscure Gaelic history and culture.

As An Lanntair's contribution to the centenary would obviously have a visual emphasis it seemed sensible to begin by identifying what relevant visual imagery existed and would be available to us. It became immediately apparent that by far the most common theme in Highland imagery is landscape and a landscape, appropriately enough, devoid of people. Given the spectacularly scenic nature of the Highlands this was understandable, but also, in the circumstances, ironic. At this point, it was decided that 'pure' landscape would be excluded in order to focus more sharply on images of the people. The diversity of images which subsequently identified themselves fell broadly into five categories. On the basis that the whole is greater than the sum of its parts, these five forms of Highland imagery became the format of *As an Fhearann*.

As an Fhearann, the exhibition, therefore grew from An Lanntair's attempt to bring this material together for the first time and see what kind of picture of the Highlands emerged. The book has grown from the exhibition. Although the pictures speak for themselves each in their own way, they are accompanied here by a series of essays by six writers, each of whom has a developed interest in the material involved.

The primary category is historical material, or images relating specifically to the significant events and personalities of the Clearances and the land-agitation. This material is not extensive, but the dramatic confrontations between the crofters and the authorities became major news stories of their time and were latterly covered by the illustrated press. The work of their artists and engravers provides an invaluable and generally sympathetic visual record which combines with other relevant material to illustrate the background to the 1886 Act. Sorley MacLean's introductory essay, 'Vale of Tears', gives a view of Highland history to 1886. As Scotland's greatest living poet and a Gael immersed in the history and traditions of the Highlands there is no-one more qualified to do so.

Secondly, there is a wealth of photographic material by both eminent professional and amateur photographers, extending from the late nineteenth century to today. These photographs not only bring together the work of such internationally renowned photographers as George Washington Wilson and Robert Adam, but also offer a chronological pictorial record of the crofting communities over the past century.

The photographers focus almost exclusively on the islands and no apology is made for the accompanying essay by Finlay MacLeod being in Gaelic. It is the language of the people represented in this book and, as he writes for them and their descendants, it is entirely appropriate that he should do so in their language. His essay considers the role of the camera as a tool of visual memory, recording continuity and change.

The third category is material which could be described as 'popular images' of the Highlands. This is material which has been commercially mass-produced, usually but not exclusively by non-Highlanders, for a market which is not always situated outwith the Highlands. This not only constitutes the great bulk of readily available Highland images but suggests a great deal

Below: *Map of Scotland* from "Geographical Fun" by Aleph, 1869. Collection of the National Library of Scotland

6

Above: *Punch* Magazine, c1900
Top right: Gus Wylie *Marion Campbell, Plocrapool, Harris,* 1970s
Below right: Sam Maynard *Oil construction yard, Arnish, Stornoway,* 1980s

about the way the Highlands are externally perceived. A grotesque but very particular 'National Type' emerges from this imagery which owes much to the Music Hall comic-turn and very little to the realities of Highland life or history. Its inclusion in this particular context highlights the distance between Highland fact and much of Highland fantasy.

Two of our essays relate directly to this material in complementary ways. John Murray is the author of the only known Gaelic Western and his essay explores the thistle-clogged mists of the 'Hielan' picture postcard. He considers the role and influence of the 'Teuchter' caricature on the image, and self-image, of the Gael.

John McGrath, Director of 7:84 Theatre Company and their legendary production *The Cheviot, the Stag and the Black, Black Oil,* adopts a historical perspective and looks at a few of the attitudes towards the Highlands, and the images which characterise those attitudes.

In contrast to the excesses of the commercial material there are very few serious artists who have focussed on Highland themes other than landscape. Fortunately they have tended to be among the most adventurous of their generation and produced work of emotional power and artistic quality as well as social relevance. The stylistic diversity of the work represented here is complemented by their thematic unity. Alexander Moffat's accompanying essay sets mainstream Scottish art in a European context and lucidly analyses its failure to come to terms with Highland history.

The final category of film and television material in a sense overlaps into all the other forms of imagery. The 'moving picture' is the dominant cultural force in our society and it has drawn on all the other elements in our visual vocabulary of the Highlands to create its own potent images. Angus Peter Campbell is a writer and broadcaster who has temporarily escaped from a successful career in Gaelic television. His essay surveys the Highland genre in films and considers television's treatment of the Gael and Gaelic from an informed and critical perspective.

The relationship between image and reality is a complex one involving a substantial element of the 'chicken and the egg'. It is not intended that *As an Fhearann* should paint a bleak picture of the Highlands and Islands in 1986. The long dark shadow of the Clearances and the traumatic distortions that followed are only one crucial element in an understanding of the modern Highlands. Despite unresolved material problems such as the land-issue, and cultural problems such as the Gaelic decline, there are grounds for optimism. Decades of institutional neglect have generated a resilience in the crofting communities, and a heightened awareness of the need for both continuity and change. Oil and fish farming are new industries being developed alongside new and positive initiatives in local government and in Gaelic education, broadcasting, publishing and the Arts. Perhaps late in the day a growing number of public institutions are beginning to recognise the significance of the Gaelic language and its current critical condition – balanced between eclipse and renewal. A new and influential Crofters Union was formed in 1985, which is already establishing a reputation for effectively representing Highland interests. These issues, however, are more appropriately dealt with in depth outside these pages.

This book sets out to scan a broad sample of images of the Highlands which we inherit and pass on. It reviews the various ways in which visual culture has responded to the people of the Highlands and their history. It also assumes that history is not concrete and fixed but fluid and open to re-interpretation and change. Hopefully it will be of some interest not only to Highlanders and their numerous descendants scattered around the globe, but also to anyone who believes that every picture tells a story. *As an Fhearann* begins with, and extends in various directions beyond, the Highland land-issue but the land, and the unresolved issue of land ownership, remains its core.

Malcolm MacLean

7

Above: J.W. Nicol (d.1926) *Lochaber no more*. Oil on canvas, 43″ × 33″, 1883. Collection of Robert Fleming Holdings

"Our places were crowded first when the neighbouring township of Mealista was cleared. Six families were thrown in among us; the rest were hounded away to America and Australia and I think I hear the cry of the children to this day."
George Macaulay, Bernera, Lewis, giving evidence to the Napier Commission

Right: J.M.W. Turner *Edinburgh Castle: March of the Clans*. Watercolour, 1820. Collection of the Tate Gallery

Vale of Tears: A View of Highland History to 1886

Many historians and writers imply, or used to imply, that England has had a relatively happy history compared with European countries such as Poland and Ireland and some more whose histories in the sixteenth, seventeenth, eighteenth and nineteenth centuries were notoriously sad; but such happiness as England's was very questionable. As a small boy I read much history, far too much of the kind that I did read, and I remember that, since I was being brought up in a most Fundamentalist Presbyterian island, my sympathies, when I read about the Civil Wars of the seventeenth century, were with the Puritan Parliament against the Episcopalian Royalists. (That did not apply to Montrose's wars at all.) I felt indifferent to the fate of Archbishop Laud, whom the Parliament executed in 1644 by a Bill of Attainder. I probably thought that any Archbishop whom the Puritans felt constrained to behead must have been some kind of monster. Many years later, in fact after the Second World War, from a review of some historical book, which I had not read, I learned that one of the charges against Laud in the Bill of Attainder was that he greatly disapproved of Enclosures. That revelation altered my view of the Cavalier-Roundhead quarrel before I came to read a word of what Christopher Hill has written about that period.

My friend, the late Iain Duff of Kintail and Edinburgh, once made a very detailed study of the history of British regiments and concluded that more than half of Wellington's troops in the Peninsula between 1808 and 1814 were Irish, because Scotland, and especially the Scottish Highlands and Islands, had had such a drain of its potential manpower in the late eighteenth century, especially after 1782, when the forfeited estates were restored to the sons or grandsons of former Jacobite chiefs. But even in the Peninsula more than half of the non-Irish were Scots, mostly Highlanders. Duff maintained from his study of regimental lists etc that not only the Highland and Lowland Scottish regiments but also many of the English regiments were full of Highlanders. About 1945 an old man from Wester Ross told me that the man who caught Nelson as he fell at Trafalgar was from Ullapool. There is no doubt at all that the confiscated Jacobite estates were restored in 1782 to the sons or grandsons of the chiefs who lost them in 1746 in order to have them, as well as such Hanoverian chiefs as the Dukes of Argyll and Sutherland, MacDonald of Sleat, and MacLeod of Dunvegan, as recruiting agents for the British army.

The estates were restored in the critical year 1782, when Britain had to face the revolted American colonies, France, Spain and Holland and had temporarily lost the command of the Atlantic. The increasing extravagance of most of the chiefs in Edinburgh and London, Paris and Rome caused them to lay heavier burdens on their tacksmen and joint-tenants, who passed these on to their sub-tenants. This move initiated indirect Clearances of sub-tenants, tacksmen and joint-tenants, who emigrated or wanted to emigrate, which would lessen the supply of soldiers for the Army and sailors for the Navy, for the chiefs and their agents could make, and did make, the supplying of soldiers the condition of continuing the tenancy of tenants-at-will. Of course, many Clearances in the full sense had occurred as early as the 1760s, for example on the Drummond estates in Perthshire, where there was no sea-coast. Where there was a sea-coast, the tenants cleared from inland straths and glens were forced into becoming kelp workers, to the great profit of the landlords. The inland landlords and chiefs had no call to keep their people from emigrating so as to have them as kelp workers, but the sea-coast chiefs and landlords had.

Thus, up to about 1820, those chiefs and landlords enjoyed the advantage of having big sheep farmers paying them high rents for the best pasture lands, and

congested areas of kelp workers on very small and poor plots by the sea. In this way they profited from the big sheep farmers and from their gross exploitation of the kelp worker. Not only that, but from among the sons of the kelp workers they could raise soldiers, and sailors too, for their own greater military glory. Thus, up to 1820 or thereabouts, most of them disapproved of emigration to the Colonies. They built great houses or added to houses already great and vied with the great nobles of England and Lowland Scotland, whom they could easily surpass as providers of soldiers for the British Army. All this has been proved with immense documentation in Dr James Hunter's excellent book, *The Making of the Crofting Community,* and it is not necessary for me or for anyone else to try to prove it further.

Before the market for kelp collapsed about 1820 there had been many Clearances and great increases of rent leading to indirect Clearances. The sheer magnitude of the Sutherland Clearances has made many forget that not only Sutherland but all the inland straths and glens of the mainland were cleared as well. Many years ago Neil Gunn gave a series of talks on the radio. Among many other things, he said that no family of chiefs who kept their lands in 1746 or had them restored in 1782 were innocent of Clearances except the Grants of Glen Urquhart and Glen Moriston. That confirmed a tentative conclusion of my own, and I remember one day coming round the bend at Castle Urquhart and seeing the steep braes of the glen green to the top and obviously still arable. How different from the other glens of the Highlands!

[Continued on page 14]

10

Top left: *Stornoway Castle*

Disraili in Sybil *referred to Sir James Matheson, whose castle in Stornoway was built with the profits of the opium trade, as . . .* "A dreadful man, richer than Croesus, one MacDrug, fresh from Canton with a million in opium in each pocket."

Middle left: *Crofting tenants of Sir James Matheson, Stornoway*

Bottom left: *Dunrobin Castle.* Collection of Wolverton Picture Library

Dunrobin Castle, the Sutherland family seat, was built in the 1840s and took five years to complete, at enormous expense. The most notorious of the Clearances took place on the estates of the Countess of Sutherland between 1811-1819. "Our grievances had their origins in the years 1814-19 . . . The parish of Kildonan, numbering one thousand five hundred and seventy-four souls, were ejected from their holdings and their houses burnt to the ground . . . the entire population were then compressed into a space of three thousand acres of the most barren land in the parish; and the remaining one hundred and thirty thousand acres were divided among six sheep farmers — who held an acreage upwards of twenty thousand acres each."
Angus Sutherland giving evidence to the Napier Commission at Helmsdale, in 1883.
In recent publicity material the Sutherland estate tells tourists that much the same thing as the Clearances "is done today by local town councils."

Below: *Interior of a crofter's hut.* "The Illustrated London News", January 1888. (I.L.N.) Picture Library

". . . The black house of a century or so ago was a grim and unprepossessing dwelling. Its walls were perpetually damp. It had no windows and no chimney, the smoke from the fire which burned perpetually in one corner being left to find its way out through a hole in the roof. The floor was trampled mud; the furniture virtually non-existent.

The crofter's cattle lived under the same straw-thatched, leaking roof as the crofter and his family. Beasts and humans entered by the same door.

In these dark, dank, insanitary and foul-smelling homes, typhoid and cholera persisted long after they had been eradicated in many other parts of Britain. And that most dreaded of island diseases, tuberculosis, haunted the black house well into the present century."
James Hunter, *Skye the Island*

Above: *James Loch* (1780-1850). From a drawing published by J. Hogarth, 1850. Collection of Daniel Shackleton

"James Loch was the great 'improving' Agent for the Duke of Sutherland's vast estates. By the time of his death, the most hated man in Sutherland had seen, and assisted in, the near-extirpation of a society, a culture and a people. Joseph Mitchell was travelling in the North at the time of Loch's death and many years later he was to write that "along the whole course of my journey through the country, I was asked in quiet, exulting whispers, "Did you hear the news? Loch is dead!"."   Iain Fraser Grigor, *Mightier than a Lord*

A REAL "SCOTTISH GRIEVANCE."

DUNCAN.—"Oh! but my mother is frail, and can't be sent out of the country in that ship; will you not let Flora and her ———",
FACTOR.—[sternly] "No, no lad—move on with the old woman: she will not be here in the way of his Lordship's sheep and deer."

Above: Collection of Museum nan Eilean

Below: Thomas Faed (1826-1900) *The Last of the Clan*. Oil on canvas, 57″ × 72″, 1865. Collection of Glasgow Art Galleries and Museums

The text of the accompanying narrative for The Last of the Clan *at the Royal Academy in 1865 reads: "When the steamer had slowly backed out and John MacAlpine had thrown off the hauser, we began to feel that our once powerful clan was now represented by a feeble old man and his grand-daughter who, together with some outlying kith and kin, myself among the number, owned not a single blade of grass in the glen that was once all our own."*

Above: *Wreck of the Exmouth.* Above right: *Recovery of the bodies.* "The Illustrated London News", 29th May 1847. I.L.N. Picture Library

The Exmouth *emigrant ship was wrecked off Islay in 1847. The* Illustrated London News *reported that "no fewer than one hundred and eight bodies have been recovered . . . dreadfully muti-*lated and in a far advanced state of putrefaction . . . and interred. Five persons, slung over the rocks by turns, succeeded in hooking the bodies in the surf; Mr. Campbell of Ballinabey and Mr. Henry Campbell of Rockside wrapped the women, all of whom were naked, in sheets and had them thus hoisted up to the summit of the cliff. Very few men have yet been found; the bodies are almost all those of women and children."

Emigration

The Passenger Vessels Act of 1803 had been pressed on the Government by the landlords, in order to stem the exodus of Highlanders who had suffered as a consequence of the changing social and economic structures. By increasing fares it had retained the landlords' labour force but the collapse of the kelp industry rendered that work force redundant.

By 1851 Highland proprietors were clearing their estates with renewed vengeance in the aftermath of the famine, and being assisted by public money made available to them by the Emigration Advances Act of that year.

Between 1815-38, Nova Scotia received twenty-two thousand Scots — the majority of them Highlanders. Two thousand left Tobermory and Stornoway for Cape Breton in 1826-27. In 1835 alone, three and a half thousand left from Stornoway, Oban and Campbeltown.

In 1840, there were four thousand emigrants from the Highlands. The following year, six hundred and thirty-one emigrants from Harris and the Uig area of Lewis arrived in Quebec "destitute and penniless". These figures hint at the scale of total emigration during this period. Many more went only as far as the Lowlands, and by 1840 there were an estimated thirty thousand Highlanders living in Glasgow.

In a memorial to Lord John Russell, Sir James Matheson stated, "Redundancy of the population is notoriously the evil and emigration is the only effectual remedy." Between 1851-53 he had cleared three thousand two hundred of the Lewis population to Canada.

On 15th May 1851, the Barlow *arrived in Loch Roag, Lewis. The factor Munro MacKenzie complained that the four hundred emigrants boarded too slowly. He sent word to the next port of call in the north of Lewis to "push them on without their luggage" as the remaining room was needed for more emigrants. An allowance of biscuits, 1lb per adult passenger, was distributed and tinware for those who could pay for it.*

Conditions on board emigrant ships were often said to be worse than those prevailing on slave ships. The fitter and healthier a slave cargo the higher the price they fetched, but emigrants paid their fare on embarking and were they to die in mid-ocean that would save on the cost of provisions and make for a higher profit margin.

Two ships which sailed from the West Highlands for Nova Scotia in 1801 with seven hundred emigrants would only have been permitted four hundred and eighty-nine 'passengers' had they been slaves putting out from the Gambia. Three out of every twenty emigrants died on board one of these ships and many others, on other vessels, never saw the Atlantic's other shore.

The sea voyages that the emigrants endured were exceedingly dangerous and thousands died from shipwreck as well as disease. In 1834 alone more than seven hundred died in Atlantic shipwrecks and in the six years between 1847 and 1853 at least forty-nine emigrant ships were lost at sea.

In November 1852 eight hundred and thirty dispossessed Highlanders left Strath in Skye, Borve in Harris and Sollas in North Uist on board the emigrant ship Hercules *bound for Adelaide, Australia.*

"The Collen (Cullin) mountains were in sight for several hours of our passage; but when we rounded Ardnamurchan Point, the emigrants saw the sun for the last time glitter upon their splintered peaks, and one prolonged and dismal wail rose from all parts of the vessel; the fathers and mothers held up their infant children to take a last view of the mountains of their Fatherland which in a few minutes faded from their view forever."

The journey that followed was a nightmare of sickness, smallpox and death . . . "Some of the emigrants are dreadfully sick . . . Some of the mothers have had their children in their arms for five days and nights without intermission".

Thirty-eight people died before Hercules *arrived in Adelaide, one hundred and four days after embarkation, leaving a substantial number of children orphaned.*

13

Above: John Pettie (1839-93) *The 8th Duke of Argyll.* Collection of the National Galleries of Scotland

"Highlanders have not yet come to appreciate the true dignity of ordinary labour." The Duke of Argyll

Below: Scottish Records Office

The chief beneficiary of the notorious Sutherland Clearances, which uprooted over eight thousand people, was the estate agent Patrick Sellar. After being brought to trial in Inverness and acquitted on a charge of murder in 1816, he left the service of the Countess to become a large-scale sheep farmer in Strathnaver and later in Morvern.

The crimes of which Mr Sellar stands accused, are,—

1. Wilful fire-raising; by having set on fire, and reduced to ashes a poor man's whole premisses, including dwelling-house, barn, kiln, and sheep cot, attended with most aggravated circumstances of cruelty, *if not murder! ! !*

2. Throwing down and demolishing a *mill*, also a capital crime.

3. Setting fire to and burning the tenants' heath pasture, before the legal term of removal.

4. Throwing down and demolishing houses, whereby the lives of sundry *aged* and *bed-ridden* persons were endangered, if not *actually lost!*

5. Throwing down and demolishing barns, kilns, sheep cots, &c. to the great hurt and prejudice of the owners.

6. Innumerable other charges of lesser importance swell the list.

I subjoin a copy of Mr Cranstoun's last letter to me upon this subject, for your Lordship's information, and have the honour to be, &c.
(Signed)   ROBt. M'KID.

Of course, not all the chiefs were able to keep their lands; and their successors, such as the Gordon-Cathcarts in South Uist, Riddell in Ardnamurchan, Balfour in Strath Conon, and Rainy in Raasay were as bad, without the protective screen of old clan sentiment, which tended to deflect blame on to the estate factors, especially if the factors themselves became large tenant farmers, as Patrick Sellar did. Not all the new landlords were Lowland. Some of them were more Highland than the chiefs, but that did not make them any better. Mull was terribly cleared, not really by the Dukes of Argyll, but by the new landlords to whom a Duke sold most of Mull in 1823. At least one of those new landlords was more Highland than the Duke himself.

Before 1829, Allan MacDougall, the blind poet of Glengarry, spoke of the great "cross" that had come on his people, how the North was utterly destroyed, and poor people, the great majority of the people, were exposed to the worst evils of lack of food, lack of clothing and lack of pasture land:

Thàinig oirnn a dh'Albainn crois,
Tha daoine bochda nochdte ris,
Gun bhiadh, gun aodach, gun chluain:
Tha 'n Airde-tuath air a sgrios.

There has come on us in Scotland a cross,
poor people are naked before it,
without food, without clothes, without pasture:
The North is utterly destroyed.

Allan died in 1829, and I do not know how long before his death he made the *Song to the Lowland Shepherds.* The word *sgrios*, which I translate "utterly destroyed", is that used in the Gaelic translation of the Bible for such holocausts as visited on Sodom and Gomorrah, and it is the one regularly used for eternal damnation.

Eternal damnation loomed huge in the message of the great Evangelical Revival that began to affect parts of the Highland mainland in the last quarter of the eighteenth century and came to the islands north of Ardnamurchan in the first quarter of the nineteenth century. Although the first two ministers in Skye who became Evangelicals, Roderick MacLeod and Donald Martin, were both of the tacksman class, the majority of the 'Men' such as Donald Munro of Skye, John Morrison, the Smith of Harris, Murdo Macdonald of Lewis, and Murchadh Mór nan Gràs, were not, and they were the Highlanders who took to the Free Church. Dr Hunter has shown how pro-crofter and even radical many of those 'Men' were, but there is no doubt that the Evangelical Movement made for an other-worldly quietude that tended to weaken resistance to the Clearances. The world was only a vale of tears. The powers that be were ordained of God; and man's real business was to make "his calling and election sure" and do his best to persuade others to do likewise. Because of this there could hardly be a militant leadership in worldly matters among the Free Church clergy and 'Men'. Indeed, there is some evidence that actual resistance to Clearances lessened as the Evangelical Movement spread and deepened. On the other hand, the spread of the Evangelical Movement must have led to a kind of contempt for the worldly landlords and big farmers; but what did happen was that some of the landlords themselves, such as Fraser of Kilmuir and Rainy of Raasay, supported the Free Church! I do not know what the great Maighstir Ruairidh said of Rainy, but I did hear (from a Mr Donald John Nicolson from Raasay) what the schoolmaster catechist from Coigach,

Above: D.O. Hill *First General Assembly of the Free Church of Scotland, Edinburgh 1843.* Oil on canvas, 60″ × 136″, 1866

A central issue of the Disruption of 1843 was the system of patronage. This system entitled the landowner to 'intrude' the minister of his choice into congregations, against the wishes of the people. "The Church of Scotland Free" was formed by four hundred and seventy-five ministers who left the established Church of Scotland in protest at landlord abuse of this legal right.

Support for the young "Free Church" was almost total in the Highlands but the landlords refused to grant sites for new churches or Manses. For many years, outdoor services, in all weathers, became a common Highland practice as the people increasingly identified with the new, radical Church and its assertive spiritual independence of the Lairds.

Below: *Open air congregation at Duthil, Inverness,* "Illustrated London News", 20th May 1848. *I.L.N. Picture Library*

Above: *Gathering seaweed for food on the coast of County Clare, Ireland*. "Illustrated London News", 12th May 1883. I.L.N. Picture Library

Below: *Searching for potatoes in a stubble field*. "Illustrated London News", 22nd December 1849. I.L.N. Picture Library

John MacLeod, said of the Free Church minister's marriage to the daughter of the big sheep farmer, Royston MacKenzie, who tenanted the lands cleared by Rainy. MacLeod regretted that the minister had not taken a bird from a clean nest.

As far as I remember, Dr Hunter has shown that by the time of the crofter resurgence in the 1880s, the Free Church had to a certain extent become a church of the Establishment; and where it was not, there was always the shadow of Catholic anti-Imperialist Ireland to cool any pro-crofter radicalism among the inner circles of the Free Church – the five per cent or so of its people who were clergy, lay preachers, elders, deacons or just communicants. Among the great mass of Free Church adherents there were widely varying degrees of confidence in the politics of the five per cent, or often great scepticism.

The great potato blight of the 1840s brought famine or near famine to the people crowded on poor plots by the sea-shore, to which their fathers or grandfathers had been forced in order to provide the cheapest of labours for the exploiters of kelp, and in order to leave the better pasture lands to the big sheep farmers. The 1850s were a time of many Clearances and they continued into the 1860s and even into the 1870s. By 1850 people were being cleared to create or to enlarge deer forests as well as to create sheep farms. Sometimes, without clearing crofts, landlords curtailed the pastures necessary to crofters. In 1865 there was a famous instance of this when Lord MacDonald and his factor took most of Ben Lee from the people of Braes in Skye and let it to one sheep farmer. Braes then was a congested area full of people cleared from Sgoirebreac, Torra-Micheig and even Kilmuir and Staffin. In 1882 the sheep farmer of Ben Lee's lease came to an end and he did not wish to have it renewed; he told the Braes people of this in a friendly way before the end of 1881. It was the determination of the people of Braes to recover Ben Lee that led to the Battle of the Braes in April 1882, for they had begun to put stock

Above: *Kelp burners, Orkney, 1880s.* Collection of Edinburgh
Central Library

Famine and Scarcity

The potato, the main subsistence crop, had failed in 1836, but it
was the recurrence of blight ten years later which brought unprecedented want to the Highlands and Islands.

"*The cottars subsist on shellfish, dulse and other seaweed, with a
little meal obtained by begging. I have seen them search the shore
all winter, even in the snow.*"

Hector MacLellan, North Uist.

"*In Mull eight thousand of the population of ten thousand sub-
sisted as much on potatoes as did, contemporarily, the lowest class
in Ireland.*"
"*In Islay, six thousand had potatoes and meal but five thousand
had potatoes alone.*"
Correspondence relating to the measures adopted for the Relief of
Distress in Scotland, July 1846.

"*I have seen the people reduced to such poverty that they were
obliged to feed themselves upon dulse from the shore . . . I see
them now reduced to such a hard condition that I can compare
them to nothing but the lepers at the gates of Samaria — death
before them and death behind them*" . . . Donald Martin,
crofter, Tolsta, Lewis, giving evidence to the Napier Commission.

"*Very much of the destitution and poverty now existing is the result
of reckless, improvident and early marriages entered into without
the slightest forethought of future consequences.*"

George Rainy, owner of Raasay.

Kelping

The Southern demand for industrial raw materials had noticeably
altered the Scottish economy by the early nineteenth century and
large-scale kelping became a major economic activity in the Highlands and Islands (and also in Ireland).

The Highland estates were re-organised and the traditional
run-rig system of land use was eradicated. The tacksman was also
eliminated and the sub-tenancy made into direct tenants and
allocated individual crofts, mainly along the coasts. This provided
the landlords with a supply of cheap labour for kelping and fishing.

Holdings were sub-divided as landlords sought to increase the
available labour force, and tenants had to use much of their income
to meet the food bill and the increased rent.

In the peak years of the kelp industry the Islands exported
between fifteen and twenty thousand tons of kelp annually, with
estimated profits of £70,000 accruing to the landlords. Whole
families were involved in manufacturing kelp and they could expect
to earn between £6 and £8 per family per season. When kelping
failed in the 1820s the Island landlords began to emulate the
actions of the Sutherland owners. People were cleared off the
estates and the land they left was added to the sheep farms.

*Kelp-making involves the burning of sea-weed until it is reduced
to an alkaline essence which can be used as a raw material in a wide
variety of products. The modern alginate industry still involves the
collection of sea-weed from the shore which is then processed in
factories such as the co-operative in Keose, Lewis. In the nineteenth
century the kelp was burnt on the shore as is shown in the above
photograph.*

17

on the mountain, refused to pay rent and had deforced sheriff-officers armed with warrants for the arrest of some considered to be ring-leaders. On the day of the Battle, a great number of the strong young men were away at fishing and other seasonal occupations and that was why women had such a part; but there were no women among those who marched on Portree on the same day to storm the jail. Although they did not get the support they expected, it was the advice of friendly ministers that really stopped them, and that within a quarter mile from the jail.

In 1874 the men of Bernera in Lewis marched on Stornoway to remonstrate with Sir James Matheson on the conduct of the factor Donald Munro; and in 1881 a rent strike was declared by the crofters of Elishader and Valtos in Skye, which made Major Fraser reduce their rents considerably. The events in Bernera in Lewis and in Staffin in Skye did not constitute a defiance of the law in order to recover lost lands, and therefore the Battle of the Braes stands out in the history of crofter resurgence as marking the beginning of really forceful resistance to the law which was being used as a bulwark of landlord power to prevent the recovery by crofters of land taken from their ancestors. Of course, the foundation of the Irish Land League in 1879 and the passing by Gladstone's Government of the Irish Land Act in 1881 stirred feelings in the Highlands and especially in the Islands. Many men from the Islands used to go as crew on East Coast and Loch Fyne drifters to fish off the Irish coast, where they learned of the similarities between their own situation and that of the small tenants of Ireland; and there too even the most Protestant of them found out that the Irish had, to an uncommon degree, most of the qualities they would like to think their own people had. Thus the anti-Catholic and therefore anti-Irish prejudices of most Fundamentalist Presbyterian clergy were often pooh-poohed by adherents of their own church who might be strictly orthodox in doctrine. When I was young there were many echoes of this in Free Presbyterian, pro-Land League Braes. Even well-loved ministers were politically discounted, especially when the Liberal conversion to Irish Home Rule made the ministers and elders Tory.

After the Battle of the Braes, rent strikes became very frequent, and, even more significant, crofters put stock on lands lost to the people before their time. There was also the deforcement of sheriff-officers and the burning of their summonses and such a resistance to the police that by Autumn 1882 the notorious Sheriff Ivory was asking the Government for troops to vindicate the rights of the Skye landlords. In 1882 Gladstone's Government refused that assistance but by that time the resurgent crofter movement was rampant in Glendale in Skye, in Uig in Lewis, in Tiree and in Barra, so that early in 1883 Gladstone's Government, torn between their Whigs and new Radicals, decided to set up the famous Napier Commission to report on the land question in the Highlands and Islands. That the Government yielded was due most of all to the militancy of the crofters of Glendale in Skye led by the famous John MacPherson, the Glendale Martyr. The Commission itself consisted of landlords, the son of a landlord, and an a-political rather Tory Gaelic scholar; but one of the landlords was Fraser-MacIntosh of Drummond, a Liberal pro-crofter M.P. and a Highland historian. Because the crofters naturally suspected the composition of the Commission, it did not halt rent strikes and seizures of lost lands.

The announcement by the Government of their inten-tion to set up the Napier Commission coincided with the foundation in London of the Highland Land Law Reform Association, later called the Highland Land League, which demanded what the Irish Land Act of 1881 had granted: Fixity of Tenure, Fair Rents and Fair Compensation. But by implication the H.L.L.R.A. had become a genuine crofter movement virtually led by John MacPherson, with active branches throughout the whole crofting community and openly demanding the restoration of the lost lands. In some cases they actually occupied them as in Glendale and on the Kilmuir estate, which included Valtos, where the leader was the Skye "Parnell", Norman Stewart, who was actually a close relative of the Nicolson chief of Sgoirebreac, who had left Skye in 1825.

Throughout the Long Island there were similar rent strikes and seizures of land, and in November 1884 a gunboat and marines were sent to Skye, the arming of the police having proved ineffective; but the prudence of the Skye crofters made the intervention of the marines equally ineffective.

When the Crofting Act came in 1886, it was better than the proposals of the Napier Commission as it largely followed the enactments of the Irish Land Act of 1881. It stopped Clearances by giving security of tenure, fair rents and fair compensation for outgoing tenants. But it did not restore the lost lands and did nothing for the great number of landless cottars. The land war therefore did not end, for the next Scottish Secretary was a Tory, A.J. Balfour, son of the man who had cleared Strath Conon. In 1887 Lewis, more than Skye, saw the greatest confrontations between the army, the police and dissatisfied crofters and landless cottars.

Nevertheless, the Act of 1886 was very important and was regarded by right-wing Liberals, Tories and landlords as a most dangerous affront to the sacred rights of 'property', which in the previous one hundred and forty years had, in the words of the famous Mull song, "made the land of the heroes a wilderness".

It would be geographically invidious to name a small number of the men who forced the Act of 1886 on the Government, though I have named John MacPherson and Norman Stewart. I have not named poets like Mary MacDonald (Mrs MacPherson or 'Màiri Mhór nan Oran') from Skye, John Smith from Lewis nor publicists such as Alexander MacKenzie from Gairloch and Inverness. Nor have I named John Murdoch of the radical newspaper *The Highlander*, perhaps the greatest of all. I may, however, be allowed to say that it was a great thrill to myself to see on a Labour party platform in Portree in 1928 the Argyll man Donald MacCallum, who was fearless in Skye, Lewis and Tiree. It was, as far as I know, his last public appearance.

Sorley MacLean

NB The next section, comprising pages 19–35, initially illustrates and expands Sorley MacLean's essay, and then continues the story of land agitation and ownership from 1886 upto the present day. The text has been compiled by the editors, in association with Joni Buchanan. The section is included in the list of contents on page 4, as "Land for the People, 1873–1986".

Above: *North Uist eviction, 1895.* Collection of Norman Johnstone

Glen Calvie: ". . . *it was the most wretched spectacle to see these poor people march out of the glen in a body, with two or three carts filled with children, many of them mere infants, and other carts containing their bedding . . .*" *The Times*, 22nd October 1845

Below: *Highland eviction.* Late 19th century. Collection of National Museums of Scotland

"*In one case it was found necessary to remove the women out of the house by force . . . One of them threw herself upon the ground and fell into hysterics uttering the most doleful sounds . . . another put up a petition to the sheriff that they would leave the roof over her house . . . and the third made an attack with a stick on an officer . . . The following year the district was completely and mercilessly cleared of all its remaining inhabitants numbering six hundred and three souls.*"

Sollas, North Uist, 1849, reported in the *Inverness Courier*

Above: *Highland Ball at Willis' Ballroom*, 1883. I.L.N. Picture
Library

*"The economical capacities of the Highlands are not to be under-
stood by a few idle young gentlemen from the metropolis, who
travel over the bare brown moors for ten days or a fortnight in the
Autumn, and then conceit themselves that they have seen the
country."*
John Stuart Blackie

Above: *Deer stalking in the Highlands*, 1880s. Collection of Edinburgh Central Library

Sporting Estates

The decade 1860-70 was a period of relative economic stability in the Highlands and Islands — the relative prosperity deriving largely from ancilliary employment, particularly fishing. But it tended to camouflage the fact that the economic foundations were still extremely insecure. "No doubt there were improvements of various kinds . . . but the people who were shovelled down to the coast were not improved; and it was not for their improvement in any shape that the new roads were made or the new bridges constructed. It was not the happiness of the great mass of the people, but the hasty enrichment of the few, that was the alpha and the omega of their economic gospel in the Highlands."

John Stuart Blackie

The transition from sheep farms to sporting estates, which began around the 1850s, continued into this period, and was a trend perceived by the crofting population as an even greater misuse of land — with their valuable grazings being given over to the sport of a privileged few.

"The arguments against deer-forests are unanswerable. What would be said in England if one or two Scotchmen and Americans were to buy up the whole of Lancashire, turn out the population, and make of it a deer-park? The thing would surely not be tolerated."

J.A. Cameron

"Why should we emigrate? There is plenty of waste land around us; for what is an extensive deer-forest in the heart of the most fertile part of our land but waste land?"

Donald Macdonald, Back of Keppoch

By 1884 deer-forests covered 1,975,209 acres of Scotland — the vast majority of that area in the crofting counties.

Come all ye jolly deer-stalkers, who hold the Highland hills
And count your honours by the heads each stout-legged hero kills,
Who gather gold by digging coal, or else by brewing beer,
And scour with me the Highland glens in the season of the year.

  For we bought the hills with English gold
    And what we bought we'll keep –
  The hills 'tis clear were meant for deer,
    And not for men or sheep.

Then come and scour the bens with me, ye jolly stalkers all,
With lawyers to defend your right, and gillies at your call,
These crofters may cross the sea but we are masters here,
And say to all both great and small, let none disturb the deer.

J.S. Blackie

Below: Murdo MacLeod *Trophies in the larder, Eishken estate, Lewis, 1986*

21

Above: *The Highlander* masthead. Collection of The Mitchell Library, Glasgow

In 1873 John Murdoch launched The Highlander *newspaper in Inverness. The newspaper gave voice to the growing radicalism in the Highlands, and was an outspoken defender of the crofter's cause in the campaign which led to the 1886 Act.*

"*The minds of the people before the arrival of Mr Murdoch were stirred up in some way, but until they heard him they did not understand their own minds so well as they did afterwards.*"
Kenneth MacDonald, giving evidence to the Napier Commission, Leurbost, 1883.

John Murdoch believed that there could be no absolute property in land. Land "was not the creation of man" and should not be treated in the same way as "houses or furniture or ships or manufactures". In Gaelic literature and in Gaelic tradition, he pointed out, there was "a distinct recognition of the fact that the land in the Highlands belonged to the clans as such and not the chiefs". A chieftain "was head of the clan or family, not owner of the great tract of land which that clan occupied". Eventually, of course, many of the chiefs received a kind of chartered right to the land of their clans, and clansmen were consequently "degraded into feudal tenants". But the fact that the chiefs had thus been converted into landlords did not entitle them or their successors to indefinite enjoyment of that status.

The Highlander *was forced to close down in 1881 for financial reasons, but the* Oban Times *carried on the radical tradition. The* Oban Times *subsequently declined into conservatism. Fortunately, the Highland radical tradition is being forcefully continued today by* The West Highland Free Press.

Above left: *John Stuart Blackie (1809-1895)*. Collection of the National Galleries of Scotland

"*John Stuart Blackie was Professor of Greek at Edinburgh University, where he played a large part in the establishment of the Chair of Celtic. Despite his pre-industrial and sometimes sentimental view of the Highlands, his dedicated defence of crofters against landlords, and his enduring championship of all things Celtic, ensured for him an important place in the movement.*"
Iain Fraser Grigor.

John Macpherson
The Glendale Martyr

Left: *John MacPherson, the Glendale Martyr*

John MacPherson was a leading agitator in the 1870s and 80s, and was one of the Glendale Martyrs imprisoned in Calton Jail, Edinburgh, following the Glendale Riots in 1883, which drove the police from the entire district of Dunvegan, Skye. MacPherson stated, "It would be as easy to stop the Atlantic Ocean as to stop the present agitation until justice has been done to the people."

Above and below: John MacPherson addresses a Land League meeting in Skye, 1884. I.L.N. Picture Library

Highland Women

Highland women were consistently at the forefront of the resistance against oppression. In the early decades of the nineteenth century they led the men at Culrain and Gruids into the fray. They "assaulted and humiliated" the sheriff-officers at Durness; in Loch-Sheil they single-handedly drove off an eviction party. In Glencalvie the women set fire to the eviction notices. Twelve years later, in 1852, the women of Greenyards (on the same estate) lined up against the militia in front of their men and sustained severe injuries.

This level of direct female activism which became a central feature of Highland protest continued in the years of the "Crofters' War". At the Battle of the Braes they were in the vanguard. J.S. Blackie described their fury and effectiveness as they pelted forty-seven members of the Glasgow police with stones and mud until,

"like the great Napoleon at Waterloo, the police were forced to forget their dignity and seek safety in inglorious flight".

Female militancy was not peculiar to the struggle in the Highlands and Islands, but was characteristic of most pre-industrial societies in conflict. It may be explained in terms of the woman's role in the family, and her need to defend the home and the children when they were under threat. The fact that women tended to stand in the front-line might suggest that it was widely thought the troops were less likely to injure women. This in most instances was a mistaken assumption. It is also likely that resistance was left to the women when the men went off on their annual trek to the South and East for work. Of course the leading role of women in the struggle against the police and militia should also be explained as a straightforward consequence of their determination and bravery in the face of intimidation and adversity.

23

Above: *The factor's reckoning, N. Uist, 1891.* Collection of Norman Johnstone

The relative economic stability of the previous two decades gave way to another economic depression in the early 1880s. Harvests were poor and the fishing failed. In 1881 the Valtos and Kilmuir crofters in Skye ceased to pay their rents, the first in the Highlands and Islands to adopt the no-rent strategy of the Irish Land League.

Below: *The crofters of Valtos, Skye*

". . . *The Irish are buying guns and will be, by the bye, shooting magistrates and clergymen by the score: and Parliament will in consequence do a great deal for them. But the poor Highlander will shoot no-one . . . I see more and more everyday the philosophy of Cobbett's advice to the 'chopsticks' of Kent — 'If you wish to have your wrongs redressed go and burn ricks' — Government will yield nothing to justice but a great deal to fear."*

Hugh Millar, 1846 (Editor of *The Witness*).

Rev Donald MacCallum (above) was born in the Craignish district of Argyll in 1849. He was the Established Church minister in Morven, Arisaig and South Morar before being invited in 1884 to the parish of Hallin, Waternish, in Skye, by a group of radical crofters connected with the Church. He became involved in the Highland land question while at University and campaigned throughout his life with the crofters in Argyll, Skye and Tiree against landlordism. In 1886 he was censured by his Church for "inciting violence and class hatred", and later that same year he was arrested in Portree. He retired to Glendale, Skye in 1920 to be near his old friend John MacPherson. His last public appearance was on a Labour Party platform in Portree in 1928, as described by Sorley MacLean in his opening essay.

"The land is our birthright, even as the air, the light of the sun and the water belong to us as our birthright".

Rev D. MacCallum

Màiri Mhór nan Oran (above), the great Gaelic poetess of the Clearances, was born in Skeabost, Skye, in 1821. Her poetry was the most forceful to emerge from the land agitation of the late nineteenth century. She died in Portree in 1898.

"Chunnaic sinn bristeadh na faire, is neoil na trailealachd air chall an latha sheas MacCalium laimh rinn."

"We saw the dawn break, and the clouds of thralldom flee away, the day MacCallum stood beside us, at the Fairy Bridge."

(Màiri Mhór nan Oran describing the Rev D. MacCallum at a meeting at Fairy Bridge, Skye.)

The Highland Land League

The Highland Land Law Reform Association was founded in February 1883, and an extensive branch structure was soon established throughout the area. For the following six years, the Land League organised mass rent strikes, demonstrations and resistance against the formidable might of the sheriff-officers, the police and the military.

The H.L.L.R.A. was "established to unite Highlanders and their friends at home and abroad in endeavouring by constitutional means to obtain for the Highland people the right to live on their native soil under equitable conditions."

Their President was D.H. MacFarlane (left), a Highlander who had converted to Catholicism and become a Parnellite MP for Carlow in Ireland before returning to the Highlands, and winning the Argyll seat, as the crofters' candidate in 1885.

"The Gaelic language has never been put to a more unworthy and unpatriotic or wicked use than when it was employed, not as a means of tranquilising the poor people by reasoning with them in a spirit of pacification and conciliation in their own tongue, but on the contrary, in urging them to rebellion and crime".

The Earl of Dunmore, January 1884, addressing the Gaelic Society of Inverness to laughter and cries of "Rubbish!"

Above: *Gunboats off Skye*

Above: *Sheriff Ivory, the Procurator Fiscal, and the Chief Constable approaching Portree on the steamship* Lochiel

Above: *Landing of Marines at Uig*

Below: *Marines on the march to the disturbed districts.* "Illustrated London News", 1885. I.L.N. Picture Library

The Land League in Action

On 7th April 1882 a sheriff-officer left Portree to serve eviction orders on a dozen of Lord Macdonald's tenants in Braes. This is the sheriff-officer's account of what happened:

". . . and at that Mairi Nic Fuilaidh suddenly cried 'Men, make them burn the summonses'. At that they yelled 'Put them down on the road'. I put them down on the road. And with the stones in their hands ready to kill me if I disobeyed they compelled me to make a heap of the summonses . . . a boy came running with a burning peat . . . never was an officer of the law so disgraced to come so far as to have burned them myself . . . that hurts me more than the stones and the clod".

On 17th April, "an imposing legal force came down on the recalcitrant crofters — two sheriffs, two fiscals, a captain of police, forty-seven members of the Glasgow police and a number of county constables". They made their arrests despite a barrage of mud and stones.

". . . The day previous crowds could be seen coming from all quarters . . . The last two contingents arrived headed by their respective pipers . . . At 12 o'clock they formed into a procession to the number of fourteen hundred and a vast number of spectators. By 12.30 they started with banners of all descriptions floating gaily about them with mottos in English and Gaelic . . ." The Oban Times, 1st November 1884.

Following the burning of eviction notices in Braes, Skye, in 1882, a detachment of Glasgow police were deployed to reinforce Sheriff Ivory's Skye police force. The clash which ensued became known as the "Battle of the Braes" and resulted in the jailing of the crofters' leaders and widespread publicity. The Battle of the Braes made a deep impression across the Highlands and Islands and the agitation escalated with the seizure of land, rent strikes, and deforcement of sheriff-officers. Police were being driven from previously passive areas and the crofters were giving every indication that they were about to repossess all the land that had been taken from them and their fathers since the Clearances.

In October 1884 Sheriff Ivory wrote to the Lord Advocate requesting the immediate despatch of a gunboat and marines to Skye, "to protect the police and assist them in protecting the property and persons of the lieges of that island." The Chief Constable had already assured Ivory that he hoped to send forty or fifty police armed with revolvers.

The Police Authority commissioned the steamship Lochiel from David MacBrayne of Glasgow complete with new skipper and special crew "in room of Captain Cameron and the Highland crew who have refused duty."

The Lochiel was soon joined in Portree by the gunboat Assistance with three hundred and fifty marines and one hundred bluejackets and the Bantever with sixty-five more marines.

This impressive demonstration of force was met with polite passive resistance as people conspicuously dug their potatoes at every township along the coast. The Glasgow Herald correspondent observed . . . "The district was found in a state of the most perfect peace, with every crofter minding his own business." The incidence of rent strikes, however, showed a remarkable rise and soon Skye landlords were faced with the consequences of not receiving any rents at all.

Above: G.F. Watts (1817-1904) *Francis Lord Napier* (1819-1898). Oil on board, 24″ × 20″, 1866. Collection of the Scottish National Galleries

The Royal Commission

As a result of the widespread agitation the Government set up a Royal Commission under Lord Napier to investigate the problems of the crofting areas. Francis Napier, Baron of Napier and Ettrick, an Anglican Tory, was a landowner and career diplomat, with considerable former experience of colonial problems and administration in India. His home address was a castle in Selkirk.

The Napier Commission examined four sample parishes — Farr in Inverness-shire, Duirinish in Skye, Uig in Lewis and South Uist. They contained a total of three thousand, two hundred and twenty-six families.

"Only one-tenth are provided with holdings which can afford sustenance to a labouring family. One thousand, seven hundred and seventy-eight are in possession of tenancies which imply a divided and desultory form of occupation. At the bottom of the social scale, more than one-quarter of the population are without land and without access to local wages."

"Side by side with this mingled multitude, so slenderly furnished with the means of life, we find thirty occupiers forming less than one per cent of the whole community in the occupancy of nearly two-thirds of the land. These thirty include a factor, a few proprietors and some non-resident tenants".

Napier Commission Report, 1883.

"There is a spirit of discontent all along the West Highlands at present and unless the government steps in and makes some concessions to the people by way of giving them the lands for which they are willing to pay, and fixity of tenure, they may be led to break the law, and a spirit of discontentment such as no government could stop. So it is the wish of the people that their grievances should be remedied, in order to put a stop to the system of oppression and slavery under which they are labouring at present."
Alexander Morrison, Stornoway, giving evidence to the Napier Commission

"For a century . . . their privileges have been lessening; they dare not now hunt a deer, or shoot the grouse or the blackcock; they have no longer the range of the hills for their cattle or their sheep; and they must not catch a salmon in the stream; in earth, air, and water, the rights of the lairds are greater, and the rights of the people smaller, than they were in the days of their forefathers."
John Robertson, *Glasgow National* 1844, quoted in MacKenzie's *Highland Clearances*

Left: *Crofters' houses in North Uist.* Late 19th century

"We and our fathers have been cruelly burnt, like wasps, out of Strathnaver and forced down to the barren rocks of the seashore, where we had in many cases to carry earth on our backs to form a patch of land . . . we have no security of tenure under the present form of land laws. We can be turned off our crofts at term day, without a penny compensation."

Angus Mackay, Farr, Sutherland, giving evidence to the Napier Commission

"The crofters cannot do without heather ropes in order to fasten the thatch upon the houses. There is one day set apart by the gamekeeper upon which you are allowed to go and pull heather to make ropes . . . you cannot attend on another day . . . or you are liable to be fined for it . . ." Murdo MacLean, crofter, Uig, Lewis, giving evidence to the Napier Commission, 1884.

"The voice of a suffering people has to be loud and persistent before it echoes in the halls of Westminster and secures the attention of legislators there."

"The history of the Highland Clearances is a black page in the account with private ownership in land and if it were to form a precedent — if there could be a precedent for wrong-doing; if the sins of the fathers ought to be visited upon the children — we should have an excuse for more drastic legislation than any which the wildest reformer has ever proposed." Joseph Chamberlain at Inverness, 19th September 1885.

". . . if the present land laws exist much longer the whole population will be paupers except the ministers, factors and landlords." John MacPherson, Glendale, reported in the North British Daily Mail, 14th May 1886.

"It was well known to many, if it was somewhat difficult to prove, that professional agitators preceded the Commission and instructed the poorer classes what to say." The Duke of Argyll.

The "Crofters' War" continued throughout the period during which the Napier Commission was hearing evidence, and the military presence was maintained until the Autumn of 1888.

In the 1885 General Election, Highlanders took advantage of the extension of the franchise and returned five crofter MPs — Dr R. McDonald, Ross-shire; D.H. MacFarlane, Argyllshire; Charles Fraser MacIntosh, Inverness-shire; Dr Clark, Caithness, and Mr Macdonald-Cameron, Wick.

The Scotsman, (30th November 1886), Scotland's leading pro-landlord paper, claimed that results were "greatly to be regretted . . . it will be noticed that in all the Islands there are a great number of illiterates . . . English to them is unreadable . . . "

As a result of the mounting pressure for land reform, and the recommendations of the Napier Commission, the Crofting Act passed into law on the 25th June 1886. It gave crofters security of tenure in perpetuity and set up a Crofters' Commission which was empowered to fix fair rents. The Act fell far short of the crofters demands, however.

A concession to the land-owning interests was that the average croft size would not be adequate for a crofting family to be economically independent all year round. Thus safeguarding the landlord's labour pool. It did not restore the vast acreages of the lost lands to them and it ignored the plight of the landless cottar population. The Oban Times described the Act as "an instalment of justice" and the agitation continued, reflecting the general view among crofters that the 1886 Act had not gone far enough.

"Security of tenure and fair rents are lauded as if they were petty divinities which Highlanders ought at once to fall down and worship as great gifts . . . What about fixity of tenure for the starving thousands who dare not touch a foot of mother earth beside them, willing as they are to pay rent for it."

Oban Times Editorial, 1886.

Crofters' houses in North Uist: Lord Napier's official report noted, "His habitation is usually of a character which would almost imply physical and moral degradation in the eyes of those who do not know how much decency, courtesy, virtue and even mental refinement, survive amidst the sordid surroundings of a Highland hovel."

Below: Witnesses waiting to be examined by the Napier Commission at East Loch Tarbert, 1884. I.L.N. Picture Library

Above: *Crofter family*, 1880s. Collection of Edinburgh Central Library

Below: *Crofter children*, 1880s. Collection of Edinburgh Central Library

THE ILLUSTRATED LONDON NEWS

REGISTERED AT THE GENERAL POST-OFFICE FOR TRANSMISSION ABROAD.

No. 2544.—Vol. XCII.   SATURDAY, JANUARY 21, 1888.   WITH EXTRA SUPPLEMENT   SIXPENCE.

READING THE RIOT ACT AT AIGNISH FARM, NEAR STORNOWAY.

POLICE AND MARINES SEIZING THE RIOTOUS CROFTERS.

CROFTERS OF LEWIS, IN THE HEBRIDES.

"Those who have entered on the path of land laws reform in the Highlands cannot now look back. In this matter they are not their own. They dare not withdraw their hand. The sunken thousands in our cities cry daily for justice which the operation of one-sided laws has denied them. They must make common cause out of their common misery. The present cry for redress is the cry of humanity. It cannot be stifled. It will continue to be heard until all the fortresses of excessive privilege and class laws are laid in ruins".
Oban Times Editorial. 27th March 1886.

The Pairc Deer Raid, Lewis, 1887

Provoked by the conversion of much of Pairc into deer forest, seven hundred men occupied the area. They carried fifty serviceable rifles and a number of red flags. At least one hundred deer were killed and the carcasses returned to the townships. A strong military and police force was despatched to Lewis, but on the third day the raiders withdrew.

Ruaig an Fheidh (Pairc Deer Raid)

We rose early in the morning — compelled by hardship —
to bring down the deer from the heights with accurate aim.

We set out on Tuesday with banners and weapons; the
day was bright and favourable, as we'll all prove to you.

Each man with his gun loaded and ready climbed the high hills,
and when a bellowing stag was seen, it was struck down.

We killed them in their hundreds, we flayed them splendidly
(and) we ate them in an orderly way, with generous portions
cunningly.

We are no plunderers, as is stated in lies; we are brave people being
ruined by want.

We have waited many days and years without disorder, harrassed
by poverty, under (the power of) chamberlains and fools.

We got no thanks whatever, we were thralls without profit;
they were set upon banishing us completely like foxes.

Our wives and children now suffer hardship; their clothes are
tattered, and they are in need at every meal time.

Our country is a wilderness because of deer and sheep, and in
spite of (high) rents, we'll not get enough to satisfy one of us.

But praise the Lord who bestowed that hero upon us —
Donald MacRae of Alness is the honourable martyr.

Donald MacRae was the great stalwart who would not yield to
the villains, although they put him painfully to the test everywhere
to the extent of their abilities.

You little old wife, full of pride (Lady Matheson), who claim that
Lewis is yours, it belongs by proper right to the majority who live in
it.

And since we have now found a chieftain, we will not cease by
day or night until we obtain the estate joyfully and honourably

Reverend Donald MacCallum, 1887

Aignish, Lewis, 1888

The following winter, one thousand men of Stornoway Parish marched on Aignish and Melbost farms — in defiance of notices posted by Stornoway's Sheriff-substitute warning of heavy penalties. They were confronted by a strong force of police, marines and Royal Scots. The Riot Act was read in English and Gaelic. Thirteen of the raiders were arrested during the fraças that followed.

The Highland land agitation and land seizures continued well into the twentieth century, most notably on Vatersay (Barra), Coll and Gress (Lewis), and Knoydart.

Top right: *Telegram requesting reinforcements to contain the Aignish Riots.* Scottish Records Office
Right: *Rabhadh — The Riot Act in Gaelic.* Posted at Aignish Farm in 1888. Scottish Records Office

POST OFFICE TELEGRAPHS.

Stornoway

TO Under Secretary of State for Scotland Dover House Whitehall London

Mob at Aignish this day large excited and determined. Thirteen prisoners captured Soldiers and Constables pelted with stones in view of other threatened disturbances I think additional force of military necessary. Gun boat and Marines preferable as accommodation on Shore is limited. Aignish stock entirely driven off while military escort prisoners to Stornoway. Copy sent to Lord Lothian Sheriff Fraser.

RABHADH.

A CHIONN 's gun d' fhuair an Luchd-ughdarrais fios gu 'm bheil Comhchruinneachadh sluaigh, an uine ghoirid, gu oidhirp mi-laghail a thoirt air an stoc fhuadach dheth Gabhail-fearainn Aignis, ann an Sgireachd Steornabha, agus sealbh a ghabhail air an fhearann: tha so a toirt Rabhadh gu 'm bheil cruinneachadh sluaigh air son an aobhair sin no aobhar sam bith eile dhe leithid mi-laghail agus ciontach, agus gu 'm bi na h-uil neach a ghabhas pairt ann, ged theagamh nach dean gach neach air leth foirneart, ciontach de bhi togail buaireas agus aimhreite, agus gu 'm bi iad buailteach do pheanas. Agus a thuilleadh air sin tha so a toirt Rabhadh gu 'm bheil cruinneachidhean de 'n ghne ud air an toirmeasg; agus ma ni sluagh aimhreiteach mi-riaghailteach cruinneachadh gu'n teid, a reir an "RIOT ACT," GLAODHAICH mar so a dheanamh:—"Tha ar n-ARD-BHAINTIGH-"EARNA, a' BHAN-RIGH a toirt aithne agus ordugh do 'n "t-sluagh a tha cruinn sgaoileadh gu h-ealamh, agus falbh gu "siochail a dhionnsuidh an dachaighean no chun an gnothuichean "laghail, air neo gum bi iad buailteach do na peanasan a tha air "an ainmeachadh anns an Reachd a chaidh dheanamh an "ciad bhliadhna Righ Sheorais, a chum bacadh a chuir air "iorghuillean agus cruinneachidhean aimhreiteach." "Gu'n "gleidheadh Dia a' Bhan-righ;" agus mar sgaoil cruinneachadh 'sam bith de 'n ghne ud, an taobh a stigh de dh' uair an deigh na Glaodhaich ud, bithidh gach neach a bhitheas ann ciontach de 'n chionta ud, agus buailteach do na peanasan cruaidh tha an Reachd ud ag ordachadh.

LE ORDUGH AN T-SIORRA.

TEARLACH INNES,

Inbhirfeotharan, 2mh January, 1888.   Cleireach-Siorra Siorramachd Rois.

According to figures published recently —
One tenth of 1% of the Highland population own two-thirds of the Highlands
Seventeen people, or companies, own 70% of Caithness
Thirty-eight people own 84% of Sutherland
Seventy-six people own 84% of Ross-shire
The Countess of Sutherland owns 158,000 acres
Cameron of Lochiel owns 98,000 acres
Lord Lovat owns 76,000 acres
The Duke of Argyll owns 74,000 acres
Lord MacDonald owns 42,000 acres
MacLeod of MacLeod owns 35,000 acres
Munro Ferguson of Novar owns 34,000 acres

"That the people who live and work on this land still do not control the land is not, however, a matter for which the men and women of the land agitation of the 1880s bear responsibility."

Iain Fraser Grigor

Top: *The Vatersay Land Raiders of 1900*. Collection of Mr Campbell, Vatersay

Middle left: Andrew MacMorrine *"Am Bochan" (Murdo Maclean)*. *One of the Lewis Land Raiders*, Pencil, 1977. Collection of Domhnull Mac'illeathain

Left: *The Knoydart Raiders*, 1948. "The Glasgow Herald" Picture Library

Right: Sam Maynard *Eishken Estate, Lewis, 1983*. Scene of the Pairc Deer Raid

Above left: *Emigrant poster, 1888.* Scottish Records Office
Above: *Poster for domestic service in Canada.* Museum nan Eilean
Left: Cherry Kearton *The St Kilda Mailboat.* Photograph, 1896
The St Kildans would enclose messages in "the mailboat" which was then cast into the sea where the prevailing currents carried it to less isolated shores

Below: *Wee Kirk, o' the Heather, Glendale, California.* Scotch Myths Archive

The depopulation of the Highlands and Islands continued into the twentieth century. The Marloch *and the* Metagama *carried off the last great wave of Island emigrants to Canada in the 1920s. These pictures show some of those emigrants leaving Stornoway in 1924.*
Collection of Norman MacKenzie

Between 1850 and 1950 the population of the Highlands is estimated to have fallen by one hundred thousand.

Above: George Washington Wilson *John Brown and Queen Victoria, 1863*. Collection of Aberdeen Art Galleries

The only published 'carte de visite' of Queen Victoria and John Brown had a third figure, gamekeeper John Grant, cut out and sold thirteen thousand copies in its first year of issue.

The late nineteenth century romantic image of the Highlands found a new, rehabilitated, archetypal Highlander in the ever-steadfast John Brown. This was the archetype that was to feature prominently in a flood of Punch *cartoons lampooning the Victorian 'ruling class' flirtation with the Highlands. The Highlands at the height of the land agitation were also at the height of fashion.*

Below: *The Clachan. Empire Exhibition, Scotland, 1938.* Scotch Myths Archive

The Scottish stand at the Empire Exhibition of 1938, which was held in Bellahouston Park, Glasgow. For this international 'shop

window' a Highland Clachan was manufactured, complete with "the Laird's Shoppe", in the heart of one of the most industrialised cities in Europe.

THE CLACHAN, EMPIRE EXHIBITION, SCOTLAND, 1938.   X.37.

There are Many Truths

Many are the poor bothies destroyed on every side,
Each one only a grey outline on the green grass;
And many a roofless dwelling
A heap of stones beside the bubbling spring;
Where the fire and the children were,
There the rushes grow highest.

Ben Shianta

"One of the most beneficent clearings since the memory of man." **Nassau W. Senior,** historian

"First Duke of Sutherland, for your deviousness and your collusion with the Lowlanders, the depths of Hell are what you deserve. I would rather have Judas by my side than you."

Rob Donn

Ideas of what really went on at certain crucial times in history usually depend on the point of view of the observer. Beware the historian who claims to be 'objective'. He, or she, will simply be trying to strengthen their position.

As in psychoanalysis, so in the telling of the events of the past, the presence and the personal desires of the analyser change the truth of the situation.

Objectivity is not a meaningless concept, but it is not a criterion that should be invoked without deep suspicion. It is not the property of the academic historian. It is not the prerogative of the richest white male person present. It is not excluded by the presence of emotion, nor validated by the lack of it. It is not proven by either articulacy nor by erudition. Its most useful function is to counter ignorance.

In this brief, and inadequate, look at a few of the attitudes towards the Highlands and Islands, the Clearances and their outcome — the raft of conscience-saving legislation begun in 1886 with the Crofting Act — I shall have no pretensions to personal objectivity, or lack of emotion. What is astonishing is the complacency of those who do claim access to truth — and the deviousness of the motion of the Vested Interest through their intestines.

The view of Nassau W. Senior quoted above is characteristic of the straightforwardly unashamed assertions of the value of the Clearances. It follows in the footsteps of the apologia of James Loch, the Sutherland factor, who argued vehemently that the removal of the people was for the economic benefit of the north of Scotland. There is a curiously 1980s ring about the rhetoric that places economic advance and profitability on some mythological level of importance, and is able to ignore the actual suffering and deprivation — indeed death — of many thousands of people.

"There could be no doubt as to the propriety of converting them — [the inland grazings of Sutherland] into sheep-walks" wrote James Loch, in his *Account of the Improvements on the Estates of the Marquess of Stafford,* — going on to say that this was provided that the people were re-settled in wealth-producing industries. This proviso was very important — but totally hypocritical. Very few were resettled in the famous model fishing-villages on the coast. Most were either left to scrape a living off bare rocks, or forced to emigrate in cholera-ridden boats. It is possible that more died of cholera on the passage to Canada than lived happily in Helmsdale, and Embo.

It is interesting that in 1986, writing in the *Glasgow Herald,* one 'Carlyle' asserted that a sure test of a person's sanity resides in their attitude to the Clearances. He went on to assert that the Clearances were beneficial in that they produced the fishing industry in the North — another strand in our culture. He ignores the existence of a fishing industry well before the end of the eighteenth century, the very small number actually taken up by the new fishing villages, and the small question as to whether these fortunate people actually wanted to leave their homes and be resettled among strangers. There is something of the white South African as well as the Monetarist about these attitudes which can only be attributed, in otherwise perfectly nice people, to the silent slither of guilt and Vested Interest at several removes through their rational capacities.

The Scotsman, of course, known in the 1880s as 'The Daily Liar', was not behind in its view of the Clearances. In an editorial written in the 1970s, it thundered:

"... for the record let it be stated that the main motive of the Sutherlands, one of the many other landlords who followed the same course, was to improve the wretched conditions of the people on their estates. A way of life was thereby destroyed, but it could probably not have survived in any case. All enlightened opinion agreed at the time the numbers living on the congested lands in the North had to fall if any economic progress was to be achieved."

The Professor of Scottish History at Edinburgh University concurred, agreeing with the present Countess of Sutherland that opinions to the contrary were the product of mischievous propagandists and 'travelling minstrels'.

Here then is one popular view of the Highlands and Islands — a miserable barren place with a population who had to be sent overseas to prevent their imminent death from starvation — the question of the profitability of the landowners' estates being of marginal importance. A view which was propagated at the time by those with most to gain from it, and supported to this day by those who have most to lose from any more outraged or socially principled attitude.

The view of the people of the Highlands at the time is quite clear, and sings out from every word that has come down to us, whether in the oral or the written tradition. There are no heart-rending melodies celebrating the joys of the emigrant-ships, or singing the praises of the 'caring' Duke of Sutherland. The two examples quoted above are only two from hundreds of such eloquent testimonies to the true feeling of the people.

Nevertheless, the contemporary historian Eric Richards, who writes with great knowledge of other sources — and with some feeling for the casualties of the Clearances, — feels able to write: "The inescapable fact is that the poor, the powerless and the illiterate leave very little residue of their lives amongst which a historian may seek material for their reconstruction." Maybe Rob Donn is not a Gallup pollster, but one would hesitate a guess that he could be a lot more accurate about the experience of the people.

There are, of course, other historians, with a different perspective on these events. The writings of the Rev Donald Sage, Hugh Miller, Donald Macleod, all contem-

Above: *The Prince of Wales shooting deer in the Highlands, 1883.*
I.L.N. Picture Library

Below: Oscar Marzaroli (b.1933) *General Curtis Le May shooting deer in the Highlands, 1967*

General Le May was Commander in Chief of the USAF when the atomic bomb was dropped on Hiroshima

porary with the events they describe, and the later work of the great Highland journalist Alexander Mackenzie in collecting and popularising these and other accounts, including a great many oral accounts, the evidence given by many old people in 1885/6 to the Napier Commission and a few years later to the Red Deer Commission, all bear eloquent testimony to the sorrow and outrage of the people.

What may be seen as a less partial view is contained in a series of letters to *The Times* published in 1848 as 'Letters from the Highlands', by one Robert Somers: "The clearance and dispersion of the people is pursued by the proprietors as a settled principle, as an agricultural necessity, just as trees and brushwood are cleared from the wastes of America or Australia; and the operation goes on in a quiet, business-like way . . . One after one the liberties of the people have been cloven down . . . and the oppressions are daily on the increase."

Karl Marx took a great interest in the processes of the Clearances, comparing them not only to the Norman kings' clearing of sixteen villages to create the New Forest in Hampshire to hunt in, but also to the German clearances or 'Bauernlegen' — which as recently as 1790 had lead to peasant revolts in Electoral Saxony. He saw what was happening in the Highlands and Islands of Scotland as part of a larger, world-wide process.

He writes: "The spoilation of the Church's property, the fraudulent alienation of the state domains, the theft of the common lands, the usurpation of feudal and clan property and its transformation into modern private property under circumstances of ruthless terrorism, all these things were just so many idyllic methods of primitive accumulation. They conquered the field for capitalist agriculture, incorporated the soil into capital, and created for the urban industries the necessary supplies of free and rightless proletarians."

It may well be argued, and has been, that the bards and the politicians and the popular journalists did not have the necessary economic awareness or the responsibility for the well-being of great estates to consider when composing their 'affecting fragments'. This is true. It is also argued that had they had such awareness they would have seen that it was necessary for the population to be 'thinned' — and that the old ways could not go on for ever. Dr Richards, for example, accuses the more emotional protesters of having put forward no alternative economic or agrarian strategy to that of the landowners.

The clear implication of all this remains that the Clearances were in fact beneficial, and that it was only 'the methods employed' which were offensive, or cruel. The fact remains that the intensive methods of cultivation of the Gaels had maintained a far greater number of people per acre than had been maintained elsewhere, that the standard of living was not the sole criterion of happiness or worth, and that although many would have indeed left voluntarily, — as they already had before the clearing began — the majority of these people did not want to go. Furthermore, the fact remains that the fertile ground which had kept so many people through the centuries was now turned into useless land fit only for sheep.

The cruellest and most important fact of all is that the criterion for the best use of land ceased to be the number of people it could support, and became the amount of profit it could make.

This new set of values led to the next development in the saga of dishonour in the Highlands and Islands — the transformation of the land from sheep-walks to deer-parks. The remnants of the population watched with mixed feelings of amusement and fear as the Great White Sheep was driven back from many parts because the estate-owners had discovered that it was even more profitable to put certain parts of their estates under deer.

Somers writes: "From East to West — from the neighbourhood of Aberdeen to the crags of Oban — you now have a continuous line of forests . . . now deer are supplanting sheep . . . Deer-forests and the people cannot co-exist. One or other of the two must yield." In many parts, this was true. The whole of Ardnamurchan was put under deer. Hundreds of thousands of acres of the Highlands and Islands became 'sporting' land.

The reason for this sudden shift in the criteria for land-use was not of a socially-beneficial or indeed of a rational order. It was the product of a new set of images of the Highlands, created around the court of Queen Victoria through the 1830s and 40s, and elaborated on with increasing skill and fantastical removal from reality to this day. This was the image of the Highlands as a wild place full of kilt-wearing neo-brigands, and crooning lassies, where a man — well, a Very Important sort of Man — could rediscover the primitive blood-lust of the hunt, could pit his wits as his Stone-Age ancestors had in the stealthy stalking of the deer, the subsequent slaughter of said deer with military precision, the blood-letting of the feared enemy in the gralloching, and the manly feasting on much fine food and whisky in the company of one's fellow-huntsmen and of course their admiring women-folk in the romantically-situated hunting-lodge, with tales of even greater slaughter at other, better times, and the odd titbit of useful industrial or investment information, perhaps even the odd deal seen through in the rosy haze of the après-massacre.

It came as no surprise that the single most important carve-up of the market in the twentieth century, that between the 'Seven Sisters' — the seven major oil companies — took place in Achnacarry Castle, a turretted mansion in the West Highlands, where the most ruthless and powerful men in the oil business assembled ostensibly to shoot grouse and fish. Apparently the shooting was lousy, but the carve-up of the world still lingers on.

Where this connection between over-fed businessmen and the crawling through the wet heather came from is a matter of ultimate disinterest but frequent astonishment, at least to me. The Victorian self-image of the near-brutish male doing battle with the natives in far-off lands, the servants in draughty mansions, and competitors on the Stock Exchange may well have found an acceptable resonance in the image of the Highland laird put around at the time with great assiduity by Sir Walter Scott in his wilder novels. The Romantic poets, or at least the vulgar image of their work — (what F.W. Bateson refers to as "The Quickest Way Out of Manchester") may also have helped to create an image of mountain life as somehow closer to nature and the Noble Savage.

Whatever it may have been, the fact is that it came to pass in a big way, and the real-estate prices in the Highlands went up according to the number of stags supported on the wilderness — and certainly not according to the number of people. And so it is to this day, with Morven, as I write, on the market as a thirty-stag estate — this method of counting, of course, ignoring the nine hundred females.

This publication is packed with these images. But perhaps it would be only fair to Sir Walter to quote his

more considered view: "In too many instances, the Highlands have been drained, not of their superfluity of population, but of the whole mass of inhabitants, dispossessed by an unrelenting avarice, which will one day be found to have been as short-sighted as it is unjust and selfish."

There are other images of the Highlands which have resulted in less drastic changes in property values. Angus Peter Campbell has written elsewhere of the twentieth-century media images. These have brought a flood of hikers, cyclists, caravanners, motorists, charabanc-tours and assorted refugees from the dark satanic mills in various stages of comprehension to the Land of Hill and Heather, on the look-out for the wit and wisdom of the whisky-drinking locals and the skirl of the pipes across the misty loch.

On the other hand the alternative images of the Highlands, as a land of girning peasants and arrogant feudal landowners grinding them under their heels has, in its time, brought a succession of open-mouthed camera-crews — mostly French — to pan over Dunvegan, Dunrobin and Dunroamin with breathless accounts of the bitter class war raging within. While these are, like the others, welcome contributors to the main plank of the Highland economy — the tourist industry — there is no doubt that political sympathy based on an enthusiasm for the might of the industrial proletariat can often go far away from understanding the specifics of the feelings of many Highland people.

While it is true that the speeches in Glasgow of Parnell and Davitt aroused a great deal of the political sympathy and organisation of the Highland Land League in the 1880s, it is important to remember that it was also the first-hand observation of the fishermen putting into the Irish ports that gave credibility to the effectiveness of such a scheme, and that the way the protests were carried out was unlike any urban strike or demonstration. The unification of the struggles of industrial worker and crofter can only be achieved on the basis of recognition of specific differences, and mutual respect for wildly different methods of organising and taking action.

The images of events and of societies are neither innocently arrived at, nor harmless. The foremost crime in this sphere of human interaction is obviously distortion, whether conscious or unconscious, of the truth. But then there are many truths, depending — as Dr Sadoc MacLeod of Lochmaddy used to say, twinkling his one eye — depending on your point of view.

And the worst form of distortion, the one from which the history of the people of the Highlands and Islands has suffered the most, is the suppression of the point of view of the people themselves. Nevertheless, this point of view exists, and even though accorded little credibility in

GROWING POPULARITY OF THE HIGHLANDS

Mrs. Smith (of Brixton). " Lor', Mr. Brown, I 'ardly knoo yer! Only think of our meetin' *'ere*, this year, instead of dear old Margit! An' I suppose that's the costume you go *salmon-stalking* in ? "

Top: Ewan Bain *Angus Og*

The popular cartoonist Ewan Bain draws on his own West Highland background for the surreal and sharply topical adventures of his cartoon character 'Angus Og' in the Daily Record.

Above: *Punch* Magazine

the history books, it is still alive in the tradition of the Gaels to-day, lingering not far under the surface, ready to burst out in recognition, as we found in 7:84 when touring the history of the Highland people at this time in *The Cheviot, The Stag and The Black, Black Oil.* The feeling, and the knowledge, is still there.

Perhaps, as this publication is connected with the centenary of the 1886 Crofting Act, it would be as well to end with another piece of 'forgotten' expression. The 1886 Act was by no means seen at the time as the great salvation of the crofter that it is being presented as

A RARA MONGRELLIS

Tourist. "Your dog appears to be deaf, as he pays no attention to me."

Shepherd. "Na, na, sir. She's a varra wise dog, for all tat. But she only speaks Gaelic."

Top: Ewan Bain *Angus Og*

Ewan Bain is referring in this comic strip to the contaminated island of Gruinard, which is still quarantined after being poisoned in chemical warfare experiments during the Second World War.

Above: *Punch* Magazine

to-day. There was no provision in it for the thousands of dispossessed, or for the restoration of stolen crofting land to the owners from time immemorial who had been driven to the kelp industry, the fishing, or to the sea-shore to collect what they could. And even to those lucky enough to have retained some patch of land, although it gave security of tenure, and a court of appeal on rents, it did not satisfy the fundamental requirement of all farmers — land that will grow crops.

Here is a translation of a song which sums up the whole story. It was written by John MacRae, leader of the Lochcarron Land League, and delivered by him to a packed audience at the Lochcarron School Hall, after the Act was announced:

> The plough is put away, up on the hen-roost,
> The land it once ploughed is empty, a waste, —
> The land of our ancestors, stolen away from us.
> If it came back to us again, we'd complain no more
> Of landlords' injustice, of the injury and prejudice
> Handed out to the Gaels.
>
> Ah then we would know exactly what to do —
> We'd drive out the keepers, and the English who
>   come here
> To ruin us and our land for their sport on the hill.
> We'd drive the deer that have taken over our
>   ploughing-land
> Up, high up on the tops of the mountains —
> And down would come Nimrod.
>
> And the sheep, oh the sheep, has been the cause of
>   great suffering
> Starvation and sorrow. It has driven many to the
>   shore,
> And over the sea. My body has known the pain of
>   seeing
> White sheep and deer nibble at the land they have
>   left,
> That would feed many and many a Gael.
>
> But the time will come when the plough will be out
>   again,
> When the garron will be harnessed and pulling
>   away,
> When the people will eat well, with cattle on the
>   hill,
> And milk in the dairy — and go no more to the
>   Caithness fishing —
> When we earn cash at home.
>
> This Bill the government shows to us, what is it?
> There is in it no word of all this . . .
> No word of a patch to plant a crop, no word
> Of the right to a place where a poor man's cows
>   might graze.
> We will not submit to it, for it has no word of what
>   we need:
> A share of the good low-lying land, to produce food
> For our children — and their children.

These words of John MacRae might serve to counter any complacent self-congratulation on the Crofting Act's Centenary. The struggle for the proper distribution and use of land in the Highlands and Islands goes on still.

John McGrath

41

Below: Margaret Fay Shaw *Four agricultural implements* (left to right): "pleadhag" (dibble), "taraisgeir" (peat cutter), "caschrom" (foot-plough), "ràcan" (rake), 1930-34. Collection of the National Library of Scotland

Above: Robert Adam *Tarskavaig, Isle of Skye, September 1931*. Collection of *Scots Magazine*

Ag Atharrachadh na Bà

Cha robh mothachadh air thalamh againn gur ann an saoghal na croitearachd a bha sinn ag èirigh suas; cha robh e dhuinn ach 'na shaoghal nàdurach. Airson uachdarain, cha robh sgeul orra. Tha fios nach eil iad cho falachaidh ri sin anns a' h-uile àite. Agus a thaobh na h-Achd, cha chuala mi ach aon iomradh oirre 'nam bhalach, ach chuala mi tric e. Bha fear de na Buidhich againn fhìn air an robh Murchadh Anna Guinne, 's bha na conastapail bheaga dubh dha. Arsa esan, "A' ghaoth a dh'fhalbh bho gàirdean Gladstone nuair a shoidhnig e Achd nan Croitearan, shad i 'An Bàn a' Ghàrraidh bho na cathrach."

Bha an lot agus a' mhòinteach agus a' mhòine 'nam pairt cinnteach dhe ar beatha, 's cha robh caochladh ri fhaicinn orra. As t-earrach, bha mi fhìn 's mo phiuthar 'nar suidhe a' gabhail balgam anns a' bhlàr-mhònach a far an robh sinn a' buain. Bha sinn a' coimhead aghaidh a' phoill, 's am barr-fhad air a shadadh is gàrradh nan trì fòid 'na aite, agus an tairsgeir 'na sheasamh air carcar a' chaorain. Bha gach nì mar a rinn ar seanair, a phòs an 1885, iad; agus fiù mar a rinn a sheanair-san iad — a phòs an 1827. Bhitheadh gach fear aca air a dhol mun tairsgeir còmhla rinn 's air cumail orra air a' chaoran, gun mhothachadh nach b'ann 'nan latha fhèin a bha sinn. Bhruidhneadh sinn air mar a bha an tairsgeir a' spoth an fhòid, agus air mar a bha am poll air a shnaidheadh, agus air mar a bha am blàr a' ruith a-mach.

Nuair a thogadh iad an sùil, laigheadh i an toiseach air a' mhòintich chiar, bhruganach gun mhuthadh — ach an uairsin air ar n-èideadh is air bascaid a' bhìdhe; air an tractar dhearg is a' Volvo uaine anns an ath bhlàr; air na feansaichean; agus air na mìltean de thaighean-geala na sgìre, mu mhìle air falbh. "Ah," chanadh mo sheanair, 's e a' sìneadh corr-fhad ri thaobh, "nach seall sibh air an taigh-solais." Chaidh faighneachd do Dhòmhnall na Sgleò, aig an robh lot air taobh eile an rathaid bho mo sheanair, an robh e fhèin air tadhal aig an taigh-solais ùr. "Nam b'ann de thaois a bhitheadh iad air a dheanamh," fhreagair e, "is fhada bho bha mi air a bhith aige."

Mar a bha na goireasan ùra ri tighinn, bhathas ri gabhail riutha chun na h-ìre gu robh iad feumail, agus cha robh cleachdaidhean no dòigh nan daoine air an gabhail a-null leotha. Bha an leantainn agus an caochladh glè mhòr an glaic a chèile; agus tha fhathast. Gus bho chionn ghoirid, bha aig gach leasachadh ri bhith air a thoirt air ais à cogadh no bho mhuinntireas no iasgach no seòladh, agus bha na goireasan ri tighinn 'nan luib. Ach chur na meadhonan ùra giorra-shaoghail air an dòigh leasachaidh sin, 's tha fiosrachadh a' dòrtadh a-steach gu coimheach, mar nach do rinn e riamh roimhe.

Bha uiread de dh'ùine ga chur seachad a' cosnadh lòn na cloinne, gu h-àraid am bainne is an t-ìm ùr, an gruth 's am bàrr — math na bà, le na bha de shaothair 'na chois. Bho dh'fhosgladh iad an toll-innearach as t-earrach 's a sgaoileadh iad na bha siud de thodhar air an talamh-àitich, gus am bitheadh an iodhlainn làn as t-fhoghar, 's an t-sloc bhuntata air a' chlàr. Agus am mìr fada mònach aig an doras. Nach math, mun canadh iad fhein, na h-annlann-sa bhith staigh.

Shìos air an todhar, 's e mar phairt den dachaidh. Stàile na bà, is spiris nan cearc, is cotan nan uan; a' chùil mhònach is a' chùil fhodair; an leth-bharaille sgadain, is na caoiteagan crochte air cùl an talain; baraille beag salainn is fear le guganan. Chan eil dealbh, ach 'nar cinn,

air an t-sòlas a bha ann, crùbadh air do chorra-biod a-measg nan ainmhidhean sin. Sabhal, 's e air a sguabadh cho glan ri cagailt. An àth 's i air a dhol fodha fo arbhar. A' chùil bhuntata. Pocanan sìl. Deireadh na sùisd 's na clèith 's a' chorrain.

As t-fhoghar, dheidheadh sgathadh gach beum, a dh'fhàs à eileadhaidh an earraich. Chuirte connlach a' choirce 'na leitear air leabaidh 's 'na shreathaig air àth. Bunan an eòrna, a' dol 'nan tughadh as ùr, an aite na bha air fhàgail air druim an taigh nuair a chaidh a' chuid bu taise dheth a chur air a' bhuntata as t-earrach. Le siaman is acair is corra-thulchainn. Iad a' cumail dion air taobhan is cleith is spàrr is cas ceangal. 'S an tobhta chùbhraidh ghorm, 'na toileachas inntinn do chearc is uan is bhalach. Na staidhraichean cloiche am balla an t-sabhail, a dhìrich 's a chrom sinn na mìltean uair. A' ruith 's a' ruith mu na cruachan anns an iodhlainn; a' cumail bad no siaman air latha grianach ri màthair no àthair, is tric fiarag air feasgar greannach deireadh foghair, 's na pocanan buntata fhathast air an lot, 's am baile air falbh a tharraing na h-eathar.

A' cheud each bàn a chaidh suas mu cheann an taigh 's a theub mo chur à cochall mo chridhe, 's an crann anns a' chairt. Le chlagan àlainn dathte, 's na brògan mar dòrnagan dorcha a' gabhail dhan talamh mar a ghabhadh e. An uairsin — cha mhòr nach canain gur ann an ath latha, ach cha b'ann — a' cheud Fordson Major le onghail is ceò is fàileadh, 's a' mhuileann slaodadh ris. As deidh sin am Ferguson beag glas a tha fhathast maille rinn, ged a tha uilebheistean mòr an IDP an impis an cur à bith.

A-mach dhan t-sabhal le mias uinnse dha laogh gligeach, faileasach, fàileadhach. A' bhò a-staigh, 's i fhathast gun am beidhir a bhreith, 's i air a cuairteachadh le gach caoibhneas is mileag a bha dol. An uairsin i a' faighinn a-mach; na crodhanan a' bragail air làr doras a' stuill. Suas dhan fheur ghorm, 's am bacan ga bhualadh, is sùil oirre a-mach air an uinneig-chùil. Ach cò a gheibheadh ga h-atharrachadh, a' cheud latha. As deidh sin, theirigeadh cuideigin eile ann. 'S an t-unns is a' chàis 'nan annas, 's an uairsin am bainne blàth ga òl as a' mhuga seapain. A' roinn gach mias gus a faigheadh gach duine a phàirt fhèin dhen bainne thiugh le spàinn mhòr, 's cnapan barra fhathast 'na mheasg. Lonaid is ceann is cuineag, 's an t-ìm mar mhil shaillte.

A' bhrùid, 's i mar duine dhen teaghlach. Chan fhaodadh a dhol gu machair gun giullan balaich no leth-nighean a bhith 'na cois ga buachailleachd. Nan deidheadh gu mòinteach, bha ris an eallach feamad a thoirt thuice, no cha leagadh i am bainne, mas fhìor. 'S i cha mhòr aig an teine anns an taigh earraich. Bu mhath leinn a' bhò ar faicinn aig an teine. Cò thuigeadh sin no sinn, ach sinn fhìn? A' falbh leatha gu tarbh, 's i ga do shlaodadh mar ite troimh bhailtean coimheach, is clann nighean air an uinneig, le gàire orra. A' bhò riabhach, 's an te bheag dhubh. 'S an uairsin am Friesian, 's aon uair 's gun dh'fhalbh sibh fhèin gu leir, de math dhomh bhith ga cumail. Mòine a-nis anns an stàile.

Na caoraich dhubhcheannach, 's iad air an sgeadachadh an dathan soilleir. Dearg is gorm is uaine, mar a bha na cairtean agus na h-eathraichean. Bho àm a' bhonnaich iomanaich gus am bitheadh a chlosaich — 'na dhòbhliadhnach muilt — crochaid air sail, thu ga leantainn aig baile 's am pàirc 's air mòinteach; troimh shàmhradh is gheamhradh. A' cheud soighle air cloimh mhìn an uain, cha mhòr mus toir instinct e sìos gu ùth a mhàthair. An dearg a' ruith sìos aodann breac: gearradh lùdaig fon

Above: *A Stornoway 'smiddie', or blacksmith.* Early 20th century
This photograph shows the door (detail below) *on which the individual branding irons for the horns of crofters' sheep were tested as they came glowing from the fire.*
Collection of Angus MacDonald

chluais taisgeil is beum fòidhpe. Fàileadh an amair dubaidh; fàileadh na h-adhairc ga losgadh le stamp. Deimhis is rùsg is dòsaigeadh, 's caite na dh'fhàg sinn pile a' phluc? An tuathalan 's an doille 's am bracsaidh. Tìde an reitheachd, tìde sabaisd nan rùide, tìde breith nan uan. Agus faingean 's an tuilleadh fhaingean.

Am muir a dh'iarr a thadhal, le lìon-mòr as deidh na langa, no taigh air a chumail 'na chorra-lòid aig biathadh is rèiteach — is sgròbadh — lìon-beag. An truinnsear le na cnapan cuimir biathaidh, 's an lìon a' dol na chuibhleagan, 's na snòtaichean 's na dubhain làn 'nan sreathan an toiseach nan sgùil. An dà bhotainn-mhòr 's an sgùil fo d'achlais, 's a-mach à seo, 's an àire mus tachair Màiri riut. Eathraichean a' tilleadh 's iad làn gu am beul, 's chan fhòghnadh sin ach crùbag no dhà airson nam balach. A' cur cruinn air na bha innte, 's earrain na h-eathar air leth. Poca marbhteach fliuch air do dhruim, a' deanamh air an dachaidh. Sgineach math èisg. 'S fhada bho nach fhaca sinn deargadh. Earrainean air na guganan cuideachd — mar a sheas sgiobadh eathar Gheadaidh ri taobh an earrain fhèin anns an dealbh a thogadh dhiubh air a' bhreakwater nuair a thill iad dhachaidh an 1912, 's na bha aig an taigh air dòchas a thoirt suas air an son.

An t-iasg is am buntata is torradh na bà; iad sin bho latha gu latha a' cumail na gort pìos bhuapa. Ach i tric a' faighinn thuca an deidh sin. Màthair ag iarraidh iasad shiùcair a chuireadh i an ceann an deoch bhùrn airson a naoidhean, is i fhèin is a bhò gun bhainne. An aon tè, a' gleidheadh cnap ìm fiadhaich ann an cnagan le duilleag chàil mu cheann — gus am bitheadh rudeigin aice staigh air choinneamh a duine an oidhche a thilleadh e bhon iasgach. "Am faca Tu i, Iùdhaich mhòir . . . ?" arsa Somhairle MacGill-Eain (faic taobh-duilleig 62 san leabhar).

Na boireannaich 's iad a-muigh daonnan, aig lot no mòine, no a' falbh dhan tobair no dhan choinneamh-sheachdain. Iad a' falbh 'nan dithis, mar dithis Kissling, no 'nan gròileagan còmhla, mar a dhealbh Dan Moireasdan iad, 'nan adan 's 'nan còtaichean dorcha, air an t-slighe dhan taigh-sgoile-dhubh. Cuimhne orra fhathast, taobh ri taobh a-steach an rathad; an cliabh-mònach air an druim 's e air a' stèidheadh mar taigh-solais. An còta drògaid, 'na dhronnag. An còmhradh 's na bioran a' dol. A-steach leotha còmhla, an teis meadhon an rathaid mhorghain. Each is cairt ri dol seachad orra, e fhèin 'na toiseach 's ise 's poca le biadh an eich, 'na deireadh.

Aite dhaibh fhèin aig na sean daoine, oir bha fiosrachadh is faireachdain ar daoine air an seilbh. Bodach le bhata a' tadhal aig faing, mar a dhealbh Gus Wylie ann an Uig. Banntrach 's i greis latha, a' dol a-mach leis a' bhò, no fiù 's a' toirt sùil oirre bho cheann an taigh, mar sean-bhean Dhòmhnaill MhicAmhlaigh, "Choisich thu crotach/le do bhata /sios ris a' ghàradh . . . " (faic 'Seòbhrach às a' Chlaich', 1967).

Sean no òg, aig an taigh no bhon taigh, saoilidh tu nach eil dad a' cur annas oirnn. Tha sinn ga thoirt air bord — air cho nuadh no coimheach 's ga bheil an rud a th'ann — agus a' cumail oirnn mar nach bitheadh sinn air suathadh ris. Bitheadh seo 'na ghoireas mar taigh, no na ionnsachadh, no na obair-laitheil. An tìr 's an dachaidh 's an teaghlach: a' bhunaid bho bheil sinn a' faighinn ar giulan. A' mhòine, a chleachd a bhith air a losgadh air teine meadhon an làir; an uairsin fàrlas is toiseach gèibhil is similear, le tocasaid bheag anns an tughadh; na pilearan geala; am modern mistress; àite-teine nan taidhlichean; a' Rayburn Casanòva, an Tiròlia agus a' Wàmsler; àite-teine màrbail bho thaobh gu taobh dhen rum. Ach

44

Above: *The Ness, Lewis, 'guga' hunters of 1912*

These hunters were assumed drowned, following a violent storm which delayed their return from Sulasgeir by several weeks. The men of Ness still go to Sulasgeir once a year and their catch of 'guga' or Solan goose is considered a great delicacy in the islands.

Collection of Angus MacDonald

Below: Donald Morrison *Island women going to a prayer meeting on a Thursday evening in the 1930s*

Above: Paul Strand *Kitchen, Loch Eynort, South Uist,* 1954. Paul Strand Archive

còmhradh na cagailte faisg air an aon rud 's a bha.

Mar gum bitheadh sinn fhathast ag atharrachadh na bà — pìos bho phìos as ùr, ach i fhathast am broinn an aon bhuaile son greis mhath. Iasg 's buntata dha ithe air a' bhòrd formica cho doigheil 's a bhathas ga thoirt às a' chlàr am meadhon a' bhùird. An guga a-nis anns a' chiste reòite. A' Volvo is ùire a thig a-mach às an t-Suain, le trèilear air earball mus bi e seachdain a dh aois, airson dhà no thrì òisgean is mhuilt a thoirt gu pàirc no fèill. An t-aodach is fhearr a rinneadh le duine — 's a thèid air feadh an t-saoghail — ann am bara aig ceann a' starain, a' feitheamh làraidh na muilne. Agus a' bheart fhèin air a ruigneachadh an dòighean air nach smaoinicheadh duine, ach fear a bha thall 's a chunnaic.

Thilleadh iad chun na cuigeal 's an crotal 's a' chrois-iarna 's a' chuibhle-shniomh am màireach nam b'e sin a bha an t-aobhar 's a' phòcaid ag iarraidh. Dh'fhalbh iad, 's cha do dh'fhalbh. Bheireadh an dòrn air falmadair am màireach cho cinnteach 's a laimhsich bodach mollach sgoth fhosgailte 's e 'na shuidhe air a bhonnach-màis.

Na goireasan is ùire, 's iad fada is cunnartaich gus ar cumail bho chèile 's gus ar casan a thoirt bhuain. Oir chan eil iad a' brosnachadh duine gu gluasad a-measg a cho-chreatair, no gus a lamh a chur ri càil air thalamh. Na dachaidhean a' dol 'nan àite dìon,'s air an sgeadachadh mar nach bitheadh duine a' fuireach annta. A' fòn ann gus bruidheann ri gach duine; chan eil agad ri do shùil a leagail air. An càr ann gus a dhol seachad air do nabaidh le fruis, air do shlighe a-mach dhan appòrtionment agad fhein air a' mhòintich, no a bhuain na mònach leat fhein. A' coimhead a-mach air an uinneig, 's a' coimhead iomhachd Reagan is Thatcher air an teilidh. Na deilbh aca anns an Express 's an Record. 'S a' leughadh 's ag èisdeachd ri cànan fuadain nam meadhonan sin, gun sgur. Tubaisdean an t-saoghail a' seòladh seachad ort, an glaoidhrich dhathach, staoin. Cha robh e a' dol a thoirt

dreachladh as-ùr air inntinn duine, sgliat a dhol air an taigh an àite an tughaidh, no tractar tighinn an àite an eich, ach chan e sin e dha na meadhonan ùra. Mar a bha le searmonaichidhean eile a bhuadhaich air an astar-sa, tha an luchd-èisdeachd — 's gu seachd àraid an òigridh — aca 's iad balbh, is iadsan a' gabhail dhaibh.

Troimh gach caochladh, tha an tìr a' leantainn. Dòchas cho mòr 's a tha ann, 's e nach leig neach a thogar ann an dùthaich 's an eileanan mar seo, an di-chuimhne iad, no an cion-suim, fhad's is beò e. Chan e a-mhàin an talamh 's an cladach 's an cuan 's an t-adhar, ach an aimsir a' slàraigeadh orra mar gum bitheadh i a' deanamh cinn-teach gu robh an smior-caillich air a dhaighneachadh anns an àite. Ghlac Gus Wylie an t-aoibhneas sin am bodhaig 's an aodann na h-ighinn òig a tha a' tilleadh dhachaidh aig deireadh seachdain, 's an t-uisge 's an gèile 'na h-aghaidh. Nach e sin a tha a' fàgail na lotaichean beaga piullach cho riatanach: chan e na nitear leotha a tha cho cudtromach ach — bàn 's gu bheil iad — gu bheil iad air ceangal nan ginealaichean ris an talamh agus ris an tìr. 'S mar sin, a' mhòine. An iarraidh a tha aig gu leòr — chan e, ach boile — gus faighinn chun na mònach, is gus am buntata fhaighinn dhan talamh. Chan e sannt no farmad is làidire a tha gan gluasad, ach miann nas doimhne 's nas falainne na iad sin.

Ann an roimh-ràdha an leabhair, 'Cur is Dlùth' (1981), thug sinn cunntas air an aite a tha aig dealbhan camara ann an eachdraidh saoghal na Gàidhlig, agus anns an latha an diugh. Tha na Comainn Eachdraidh air trusadh féumail a dheanamh air dealbhan a thogadh an studios, far am bheil teaghlaichean no caraidean air an togail còmhla ri chèile. A' thuilleadh air a-sin, tha luchd camara air a bhith a' tighinn a dhealbhadh an àite bho chionn greis mhòr a-nis, agus tha an obair aca cho cudtromach dhan chultur ri modh-ealain a tha againn. Tha an dealbh dubh is geal, gu h-àraid, cho socair, fìr, is modhail.

Tha sinn air fàs cho eolach air na dealbhan àlainn aig Washington Wilson 's gu saoil sinn gun aithnich sinn na Sgitheanaich ud a-muigh ag obair air an earrach. Bha e, mar a bha gu leòr a thàinig as a dhèidh, air a bheò-ghlacadh le na h-ionnstramaid oibreach a bha aig na daoine, agus le dreach is cumadh na tìr. Thug e a' chas-chrom da-riribh a-steach a shaoghal nan ealain. Agus a' chlach-bhrà. Daoine 'nan seasamh aig an doras, gan sealltainn fhein ann an solas an latha. Ach gàire math air lethcheann an fhir a tha a' toirt sùil air a phiuthar 's i fon chliabh-feamad airson math a' chamara.

Mairead Fay Shaw a fhuair cho faisg air na daoine, 's sin faicsinneach air mar a nochd iad iad-fhein dhi anns na dealbhan a thog i còmhla riutha. Bha i a' ceangal nan daoine ri an obair làitheil, 's iad le cnocan no clò 'nan uchd, no le an cas air cuibhle-shniomh. Ged a thog i dealbhan troimh na h-Eileanan an Iar air fad, 's ann an Uibhist a Deas a rinn i a' chuid bu mhotha 's a b'fheàrr.

Bho chionn fhada bha iarraidh agam gu nochdadh dealbhan miorbhaileach Robert Adam, agus tha iad againn a-nis. Cò eile a ghlac raon cho farsaing, 's a sheall mar a tha na daoine 's an ainmhidh 's an obair mar phàirt iomlan dhen àite? Tha gestalt anns na dealbhan aige a tha gan cur air leth. Tha an dhealbh den chreaga aig ceann a-stigh na Clif an Uig cho fosgailte, soilleir, làidir ri iomhaigh a chaidh a ghlacadh fhathast.

Tha Kissling a' toirt am follais nan liutan a bha aig na daoine, 's mar a bha na sgilean aca gan nochdadh fhein anns na bha iad a' deanamh. Gan glacadh, cuideachd, mus deidheadh iad an di-chuimhne. Rudeigin mar a

chaidh na h-òrain a chruinneachadh. Tha an dà-chuid sin anns na dealbhan aig Dan Moireasdan, agus taobh is daimh ri gach duine a thog e, oir bha e eòlach is faisg air gach duine aca 'na èirigh suas.

Thàinig Paul Strand à staball Stieglitz an New York, agus thug esan alt na h-oibreach seo gu ìre cho ard 's ghabhadh deanamh. Lorg is neartaich e uaisleachd is daonnachd nan daoine, 's chan fhaic sinne ealain a thig gu foirfe nas àirde na'n obair aige. Bidh buaidh aige air dealbhan gach duine a thig a seo airson ùine mhòr.

Tha Gus Wylie a' sireadh is a' nochdadh nan atharraichean a tha a' tighinn air dòigh-beatha an àite, ach tha na dealbhan aige a' dol nas fhaide na sin. Tha iad cuideachd ri cur dreach air na nithean is laidir 's is tarraingich anns a' chultur fhèin. Agus a-rithist, tha cruth is gnè nan daoine aig cridhe na tha sin. Tha Sam Maynard, e fhèin, a' fighe phàtarain ghrinn à farsaingeachd na tìr, agus mar a tha na daoine a' gluasad is ag obair.

Ann am Murchadh MacLeoid tha dealbhadair òg againn às an àite fhèin. Tha na h-Eileanan an Iar, 's na tha unnta, ri fosgladh a-mach dha, agus tha e fhèin mar phàirt dhiubh. Cha robh samhail seo ann gu seo fhèin: fear ealain òg a thogadh anns an àite, mu thràth a' cumail sgàthan ris an àite. Tha an eadar-theangachadh aige fileanta agus fialaidh. Agus is coltach gu bheil fios aige cho prìseil is a tha a leithid anns a' chultur a tha seo, an dràsda.

Ann an cèis nan ceud bliadhna tha an gleidheadh is an t-atharrachadh a' nochdadh anns na tha againn de dhealbhan. Cumaidh na h-aodainn agus na cnuic orra, troimh na tha ri thighinn — gus bith de mar a thig caochladh air na goireasan, is mar a bhitheas iad mu ar timcheall. Thig an wigwam a' aite an rùdhain, is cha aithnicheadh mo sheanair e. Ach cruth is iomhaigh nan daoine: is iomadh negative tron tig iad fhathasts.

Fionnlagh MacLeòid

Above: Gus Wylie *Schoolgirl returning home, 1970s*

A schoolgirl returning home to Skye for the weekend. Many island school children spend their middle and senior years of secondary school in hostels or lodgings. Senior pupils from the Uists spend their school years living away from their families and only get home at holiday time.

The only sixth-year secondary school in the Western Isles is in Stornoway. However, the first six-year secondary in the Uists is currently under construction at Liniclete.

Below: Gus Wylie *Seaweed gatherer, Ardvule Point, South Uist, 1970s*

Above: Wernhar Kissling *Two women walking home in the evening, Eriskay*, 1936. Collection of the School of Scottish Studies

Below: Donald Morrison *Going to 'lift' peats, and carrying a sack of hay for the horse*, 1930s

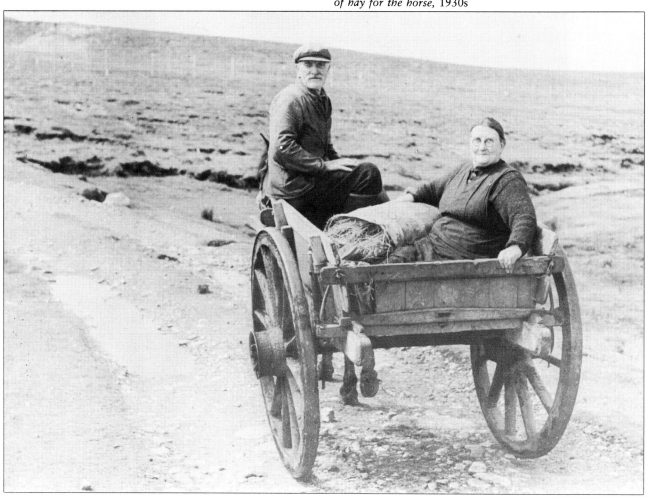

Above: Wernhar Kissling *Family group, 'blackhouse' interior, Polachar, South Uist,* 1934. Collection of the School of Scottish Studies

The Crofter and the Camera

The elements of continuity and change which have been a normal part of the crofter's life during the last century have provided ready material for photographic images. While some photographers have stressed the lasting traditions, others have delighted in counterpointing cultural innovations against unchanging features of people and place. Others have tended more towards the ethnographic, and have concerned themselves with recording the details of implements, customs and skills, lest these should disappear before this could be done.

From the earliest images of George Washington Wilson, the crofter has been taken out to stand at the door while holding a creel or cas-chrom. His wife sits nearby with one foot on her spinning wheel, and busily carding or displaying a sieve. All articles are home-made and the feel of ethnicity is strong. The Skye group of crofters with their Spring implements and torn clothes and clay pipe have become as familiar and dear to us as if we had known them. Their task and posture are ones we still know.

Later, around 1930, Margaret Fay Shaw compiled portraits of the Uist crofters in much the same tradition. Her people are always busy at something, as I am sure they would have been. Her interiors give an intimate feel of the place, and her pictures are precious as an account of Hebridean crofters in their surrounding at that time.

Dan Morrison's photographs of the people of Ness in Lewis are concerned with their everyday work. His are clear and simple accounts of people as he met them in the villages. There is an element of encounter in many of his pictures, and the feeling that the picture is but a part of that encounter. Sam Maynard and Oscar Marzaroli have a similar tendency — to be out and about and to catch the image on the wing. Often with dramatic, and sometimes amusing, effect.

Kissling was clearly engrossed by the skills and tools of the crofters he got to know. He does not give us the image of a quern by itself, as a symbol of man's achievement: he likes the man's hand to be there, to show us how he works it. His method of making sequences of pictures is a fore-runner of film and video.

In Paul Strand we have the zenith of the art, expressed in Hebridean images. The crofting life could not have been depicted with more immediacy and strength, and the lives of the people reflected in forms which gave expression to their warmth and dignity. Strand's humanism is evident in the way he enabled the Uist people to present themselves with ease and a sense of fulfilment.

Where artists such as Kissling went for the close detail, Robert Adam stood back and compiled his long-shots so as to hold in balance as much of the landscape and its people as the frame could contain. His images have a gestalt all of their own. While being very interested in land use, and having depicted the way in which the crofter relates to, and adapts, his piece of land, Adam's portraits of the people themselves, and of the villages they inhabit, are outstanding.

Where the horse and the creel and the cas-chrom and the black-house were made important visual metaphors of crofting life by these earlier artists, new symbols dominate the narrative now. The lasting features of the landscape and the people still provide the legend, but the tractor and the mobile shop and the peats and the sheep have become the new icons. This change reflects, among other things, how the crofter's use of the land has altered during this period. It is not merely a matter of new tilling implements having been introduced: tilling, itself, has a minor place in the profile of crofting routine.

Gus Wylie delineates Hebridean life very much in the new terms. The crofter is now in his place, either on his tractor or attending to some part of the sheep-cycle, at a fank. Or at his modern loom. Wylie has succeeded with remarkable skill in creating images which capture the modern crofter as he incorporates change into ancient elements of his life-style.

Murdo MacLeod, from Shawbost in Lewis, counterpoints incoming influences and existing values and behaviour. He himself is changing as he attempts to define his childhood's culture. He seeks for illuminating contrasts between the past and the present, as well as between different regions within his native Hebrides. His keen awareness of the contrasting influence of church and television is likely to remain a significant part of his work for some time. He is the youngest of the photographers.

Photographic interpretation of the crofting lives of Highlanders and Islanders has become an important means of expression, both for the artist and for the people whose ways and setting are being defined. It is not merely a record of the changes, but — at its best — a continuing attempt to catch the essence of what it is to be a crofter, and a Gael.

Finlay MacLeod

Top: Oscar Marzaroli *The salmon fishermen, Skye, 1970*

Middle right: *Herring girls, Ullapool, c1890*

Bottom right: *Lewisman with spoon net, 1930s*

Left: George Washington Wilson *Castlebay, Barra, 1880s*
The lecture notes accompanying this lantern slide read . . . "The Island of Barra is separated from South Uist by the Sound of Barra, full of rocks and shoals. At the southern end of the island is the land-locked harbour of Castlebay at which steamers regularly call.
When herring shoals are off the coast, the whole place resounds with stir, the air is laden with the odour of decaying fish, and the village of Castlebay thronged with the fishermen of the fleet."

Top left: Donald Morrison *Woman with peat creel*, 1930s

Above: Donald Morrison *Returning from the well*, 1930s

Bottom left: Donald Morrison *A Ness man giving his friend a haircut*, 1930s

Below: Donald Morrison *Taking peats to the road*, 1930s

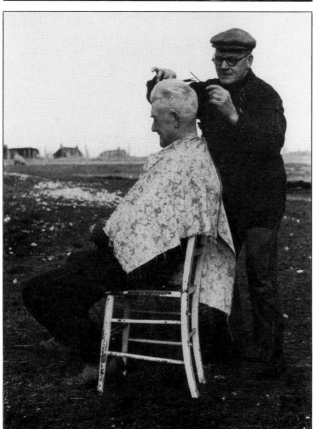

Above: Wernhar Kissling *Creel making, Garrynamonie, South Uist*, 1947. Collection of the School of Scottish Studies
Below: Wernhar Kissling *Duncan MacDonald of Peninerine, South Uist, the famous Gaelic story-teller*, 1953. Collection of the School of Scottish Studies

Below: Wernhar Kissling *Gathering crotal, Loch Carnan, South Uist*, Collection of the School of Scottish Studies
Crotal is used as a foundation in tweed of nearly every colour.

Above: Wernhar Kissling *Thatching, Eriskay*, 1936. Collection of the School of Scottish Studies

Soaked in peaty water when boiled and washed, crotal-dyed wool gives the tweed its distinctive smell

Left: Margaret Fay Shaw *Mrs Alasdair Currie, South Uist*, 1930-34
"Mrs Alasdair Currie twists her wool on a spindle or 'fearsaid'. She wears a hand-knitted shawl and 'drocaid' skirt."
Collection of the National Library of Scotland
Above: Margaret Fay Shaw *Hallowe'en, South Uist*, 1930. Collection of the National Library of Scotland
Below: Margaret Fay Shaw *Man making heather rope*, 1931-34. Collection of the National Library of Scotland

Above: Robert Adam *Uig Croft, Timsgarry, West Lewis, 9th April, 1938*. Collection of *Scots Magazine*

Below: Robert Adam *Valtos, West Lewis, April 1938*. Collection of *Scots Magazine*

Above: Paul Strand (1890-1973) *Ewan MacLeod, South Uist,* 1954. Paul Strand Archive

Above: Paul Strand *Margaret Maclean, South Uist,* 1954. Paul Strand Archive

Below: Paul Strand *Archie MacDonald, South Uist,* 1954. Paul Strand Archive

Below: Paul Strand *Neil MacDonald, South Uist,* 1954. Paul Strand Archive

Above: Oscar Marzaroli *The Cockle Strand, Barra,* 1964

Below: Oscar Marzaroli *Mobile Shop, Lewis,* 1980

Above: Gus Wylie (b. 1935) *Boatbuilder, Ness, Lewis, 1970s*

Below: Gus Wylie *Murchadh MacPharlain, the Melbost Bard, Lewis, 1970s*
The late Murdo MacFarlane was a staunch defender of the Gaelic language and culture and an outspoken opponent of the new NATO Base. *Gus Wylie writes that as he set up his tripod to take this shot Murdo patted the wall with his hand. "You see this wall", he said, "this is as far as the Gaelic decline is going."*

Above: Sam Maynard (b.1958) *Man moor burning, Lewis, 1985*

Below: Sam Maynard *Peat cutting machine, Lewis, 1985*
Most peat cutting in the islands is still done in the traditional way although the Irish Government has developed this natural resource to fuel peat power-stations.

Below: Sam Maynard *Carloway Cattle Show, Lewis, 1985*

Above: Murdo MacLeod (b. 1964) *Funeral, Dalmore, Lewis, 1986*

"Most of us in the islands are born and brought up by the sea. On cold, gusty, salt days men come in a quiet slow procession. Individually they stray away to stand by the graves of those they've buried before. They speak quietly and hope it doesn't rain on their impractical Sunday suits. To the rush of the Atlantic and the bleating of sheep they shovel the sand, stamp down the clods on another friend by the sea." Murdo MacLeod, 1986

Below: Murdo MacLeod *Comhairle nan Eilean Education Committee meeting, 1986*

Above: Murdo MacLeod *Hunter being congratulated by the head
gamekeeper, Eishken Estate, Pairc, Lewis, 1986*

Nuair Bha Mi Og

. . . Toirt 'na mo chuimhn' iomadh nì a rinn mi,
nach faigh mi 'm bann gu ceann thall mo sgeòil –
a' falbh sa gheamhradh gu luaidh is bainnsean,
gun solas lainnteir ach ceann an fhòid;
bhiodh òigridh ghreannmhor ri ceòl is dannsa,
ach dh'fhalbh an t-àm sin 's tha'n gleann fo bhròn –
bha'n tobht' aig Anndra 's e làn de dh'fheanntaig
toirt 'na mo chuimhne nuair bha mi og.

Nuair chuir mi cuairt air gach gleann is cruachan
far 'n robh mi suaimhneach a' cuallach bhò,
le òigridh ghuanach tha nis air fuadach
de shliochd na tuath bha gun uaill, gun ghò –
na raoin 's na cluaintean fo fhraoch is luachair
far 'n tric a bhuaineadh leam sguab is dlòth,
's nam faicinn sluagh agus taighean suas annt',
gu fàsainn suaimhneach mar bha mi òg.

Màiri Nighean Iain Bhàin
(Màiri Mhór nan Oran)

When I Was Young

. . . It reminded me of many things I had done,
some of which I shall not gather in until the end of my
days –
going to waulkings and weddings in winter,
not with lantern light but with a burning peat;
lively youngsters engaged in music and dancing then,
but that time has gone and the glen is saddened;
the ruins of Andrew's house, overgrown with nettles,
reminded me of when I was young.

When I had walked round each glen and small hill
where I had once lived without care, herding cows,
with light-hearted young people who have now been
driven away,
descendants of native folk who were free of vanity and
guile –
the fields and pastures covered in heather and rushes
where I'd often cut sheaves and small bundles of corn,
and if I were to see people there and houses built,
I would become as carefree as when I was young.

Mary MacPherson
(Màiri Mhór nan Oran)

From *Màiri Mhór nan Oran,* ed. Dòmhnall Eachann
Meek, Gairm, Glaschu 1977

Ban-Ghàidheal

Am faca Tu i, Iùdhaich mhóir,
ri'n abrar Aon Mhac Dhé?
Am fac' thu a coltas air Do thriall
ri stri an fhion-lios chéin?

An cuallach mheasan air a druim,
fallus searbh air mala is gruaidh;
's a' mhìos chreadha trom air cùl
a cinn chrùibte, bhochd, thruaigh.

Chan fhaca Tu i, Mhic an t-saoir,
ri'n abrar Rìgh na Glòir,
am measg nan cladach carrach siar,
fo fhallus cliabh a lòin.

An t-earrach so agus so chaidh
's gach fichead earrach bho 'n tùs
tharruing ise an fheamainn fhuar
chum biadh a cloinn is duais an tùir.

Is gach fichead foghar tha air triall
chaill i samhradh buidh nam blàth;
is threabh an dubh chosnadh an clais
tarsuinn mìnead ghil a clàir.

Agus labhair T'Eaglais chaomh
mu staid chaillte a h-anama thruaigh;
agus leag an cosnadh dian
a corp gu sàmhchair dhuibh an uaigh.

Is thriall a tìm mar shnighe dubh
a' drùdhadh tughaidh fàrdaich bochd;
mheal ise an dubh chosnadh cruaidh;
is glas a cadal suain an nochd.

Somhairle MacGill-Eain

Highland Woman

Has Thou seen her, great Jew,
who art called the One Son of God?
Hast Thou, on Thy way, seen the like of her
labouring in the distant vineyard?

The load of fruits on her back,
a bitter sweat on brow and cheek;
and the clay basin heavy on the back
of her bent, poor, wretched head.

Thou hast not seen her, Son of the carpenter,
who art called the King of Glory,
among the rugged western shores
in the sweat of her food's creel.

This spring and last
and every twenty springs from the beginning
she has carried the cold seaweed
for her children's food and the castle's reward.

And every twenty autumns that have gone
she has lost the golden summer of her bloom;
and the black-labour has ploughed the furrow
across the white smoothness of her forehead.

And Thy gentle Church has spoken
of the lost state of her miserable soul;
and the unremitting toil has lowered
her body to a black peace in a grave.

And her time has gone like a black slush
seeping through the thatch of a poor dwelling;
the hard black-labour was her inheritance;
grey is her sleep tonight.

Sorley MacLean
Translated from the author's own Gaelic

From *Dain do Eimhir* MacLellan, Glasgow 1943

Hallaig

"Tha tìm, am fiadh, an coille Hallaig"

Tha bùird is tàirnean air an uinneig
troimh'm faca mi an Aird an Iar
's tha mo ghaol aig Allt Hallaig
'na craoibh bheithe, 's bha i riamh

eadar an t-Inbhir 's Poll a' Bhainne,
thall 's a bhos mu Bhaile-Chùirn:
tha i 'na beithe, 'na calltuinn,
'na caorunn dhìreach sheang ùir.

Ann an Screapadal mo chinnidh,
far robh Tarmad 's Eachunn Mór,
tha'n nigheanan 's am mic 'nan coille
ag gabhail suas ri taobh an lóin.

Uaibhreach a nochd na coilich ghiuthais
ag gairm air mullach Cnoc an Rà,
direach an druim ris a' ghealaich —
chan iadsan coille mo ghràidh.

Fuirichidh mi ris a' bheithe
gus an tig i mach an Càrn,
gus am bi am bearradh uile
o Bheinn na Lice f'a sgàil.

Mura tig 's ann theàrnas mi a Hallaig
a dh'ionnsaigh sàbaid nam marbh,
far a bheil an sluagh a' tathaich,
gach aon ghinealach a dh'fhalbh.

Tha iad fhathast ann a Hallaig,
Clann Ghill-Eain 's Clann MhicLeòid,
na bh'ann ri linn Mhic Ghille-Chaluim:
Chunnacas na mairbh beò.

Somhairle MacGill-Eain

Hallaig

"Time, the deer, is in the wood of Hallaig"

The window is nailed and boarded
through which I saw the West
and my love is at the Burn of Hallaig,
a birch tree, and she has always been

between Inver and Milk Hollow,
here and there about Baile-chuirn:
she is a birch, a hazel,
a straight, slender young rowan.

In Screapadal of my people
where Norman and Big Hector were,
their daughters and their sons are a wood
going up beside the stream.

Proud tonight the pine cocks
crowing on the top of Cnoc an Ra,
straight their backs in the moonlight —
they are not the wood I love.

I will wait for the birch wood
until it comes up by the cairn,
until the whole ridge from Beinn na Lice
will be under its shade.

If it does not, I will go down to Hallaig,
to the Sabbath of the dead,
where the people are frequenting,
every single generation gone.

They are still in Hallaig,
MacLeans and MacLeods,
all who were there in the time of Mac Gille Chaluim:
the dead have been seen alive.

Sorley MacLean

Translated from the author's own Gaelic
From *Reothairt is Contraigh (Spring tide and Neap tide)*,
Canongate, Edinburgh 1977

Srath Nabhair

Anns an adhar dhubh-ghorm ud,
àirde na sìorraidheachd os ar cionn,
bha rionnag a' priobadh ruinn
's i freagairt mireadh an teine
ann an cabair taigh m' athar
a' bhlianna thugh sinn an taigh le bleideagan sneachda.

Agus siud a' bhlianna cuideachd
a shlaod iad a' chailleach don t-sitig,
a shealltainn cho eòlach 's a bha iad air an Fhìrinn,
oir bha nid aig eunlaith an adhair
(agus cròthan aig na caoraich)
ged nach robh àit aice-se anns an cuireadh i a ceann
                                                    fòidhpe.

A Shrath Nabhair 's a Shrath Chill Donnain,
is beag an t-iongnadh ged a chinneadh am fraoch àlainn
                                                    oirbh,
a' falach nan lotan a dh' fhàg Pàdraig Sellar 's a sheòrsa,
mar a chunnaic mi uair is uair boireannach cràbhaidh
a dh'fhiosraich dòrainn an t-saoghail-sa
is sìth Dhé 'na sùilean.

Ruaraidh MacThòmais

Strathnaver

In that blue-black sky,
as high above us as eternity,
a star was winking at us,
answering the leaping flames of fire
in the rafters of my father's house,
that year we thatched the house with snowflakes.

And that too was the year
they hauled the old woman out to the dung-heap,
to demonstrate how knowledgeable they were in
                                                    Scripture,
for the birds of the air had nests
(and the sheep had folds)
though she had no place in which to lay her head.

O Strathnaver and Strath of Kildonan,
it is little wonder that the heather should bloom on your
                                                    slopes,
hiding the wounds that Patrick Sellar, and such as he,
                                                    made,
just as time and time again I have seen a pious woman
who has suffered the sorrow of this world,
with the peace of God shining from her eyes.

Derick Thomson

Translated from the author's own Gaelic
From *Creachadh na Clàrsaich*, Macdonald Publishers,
Edinburgh 1982

Above: James Guthrie (1859-1930) *A Highland Funeral*. Oil on canvas, 51″ × 76″, 1882. Collection of Glasgow Art Galleries and Museums

Below: Joseph Farquarson (1846-1935) *The Box Bed, Croft Interior*. Oil on canvas, 14″ × 21″, 1874. Collection of Aberdeen Art Gallery

Beyond The Highland Landscape

The vast majority of paintings about the Scottish Highlands conform to a certain type. Those paintings can generally be called Romantic in conception and depict natural phenomena such as rugged mountains, misty glens, and remote lochs. Some are remarkable for their imaginative fusion of poetry and fantasy, as they seek to express something of the relationship between man and nature; on the other hand, many are merely picturesque, lacking in the realm of feeling and in the quality of vision necessary to translate such awe-inspiring material into significant works of art. It is important to remember that this view of the Highlands is a nineteenth century one, imposed by lowlanders such as Sir Walter Scott and English artists like Turner, and it is one which still persists today. Alongside the romantic associations of Highland landscape has grown (in more popular art forms) a comical view of the way of life in the Highlands, with grouse shooting, bagpipes, and clan gatherings well to the fore. There is no doubt that a combination of both these views has gone into the creation of a kind of image which attracts many of the two million annual tourists to these remote regions of Scotland. But what if we look beyond this facade at the complex social realities of the real Highlands and ask if this has been a suitable subject for art and artists. Has an image of the people of the Highlands truly emerged since the passing of the Crofting Act in 1886?

The past hundred years has been a century of accelerated political, cultural, and artistic change. The modern movement in the visual arts developed in the great capital cities of Europe between 1880 and 1914 and after the First World War, before becoming established as the cultural status quo in both Western Europe and America. Mainly concerned with aesthetic and formal ideas, Modernism exalted the mechanical age and a specific idea of progress. Old traditions were denounced as utopias abounded. A wide variety of different movements and styles were thrown up, each succeeding or replacing each other with extreme rapidity, causing a fundamental change in the function of art and in the role of the artist. The modern artist was no longer chiefly concerned with the representation of the real world. He was also no longer interested in provincial or rural themes.

"The great decisions on the development of modern art were made in France. What took shape in France in the first half of the nineteenth century developed in the second half with an intensity, complexity and rapidity unknown in art history since the time of the Renaissance."[1]

In the middle years of the nineteenth century, rural subject-matter in the paintings of Millet and Courbet had become the basis of a radical art, linked to the progressive social forces of the time. Millet's peasant naturalism reflected the need for art to deal with contemporary life, and this in turn met the need for new ideas in art – ideas which became closely associated with new aspirations in society.[2] The peasant became a controversial subject as rural depopulation and the plight of the peasant became a critical social issue. In 1789 the population of France was twenty-seven million, of whom twenty-two million were peasants. After the revolution of 1848, the peasant exodus to the cities increased and by 1900 there were only eight million French peasants. No longer did they die of famine; instead they were forced to desert the

Above: *For Auld Lang Syne*. Publisher unknown. Scotch Myths Archive

village in order to become wage earners. Millet elevated the peasant and his labour onto an heroic scale, thus making paintings which were unsettling and provocative. Courbet's great paintings of this period, *The Stonebreakers* and *Burial at Ornans*, also deal intentionally with rural themes. Again, by painting contemporary life and by elevating the common man to the rank of history painting, Courbet's paintings were perceived to be disturbing and threatening. Both artists had depicted rural life at a moment of immense social change. Thereafter the peasant was never again to occupy such a prominent political role in Western Europe. In the later years of the nineteenth century the peasant became a sentimental figure in art, appropriated by bourgeois salon painters as a symbol of an untouched and simple past way of life.

Although the revolutionary potential of rural subject-matter subsided after the mid-century, with the peasant being replaced by the new urban proletariat as the major focus for radical statements about the nature of capitalist society, certain aspects of Millet's work and ideals were inherited and developed by Van Gogh and Gauguin. They, too, rejected urban civilisation, preferring what they saw as the dignity and down-to-earth manners of rural existence. This is surely the beginning of the cult of the primitive in modern painting, and perhaps one of the last attempts by the avant-garde to seek such inspiration in remote parts of Europe. Gauguin would soon go off to the South Seas, whilst Picasso and others would later turn to African sculpture.

This relationship between 'primitive' and 'civilised' worlds remains an ongoing and uneasy undercurrent in modern art. The wish to embrace primitive modes of life or forms of art could easily be interpreted as an escape from our urban environment. On the other hand it could be seen as an attempt to question seriously the false values of Western civilisation in an endeavour to re-create a new kind of organic unity between art and society. Although the peasant is scarcely a truly 'primitive' figure, he has remained as an alternative to the modern industrial world. The mythic status of the rural labourer has continued to prove a potent symbol in modern art,[3] standing for the ideals of honest labour as opposed to the soul-less degradation of work on the factory floor, though it must be said that to portray rural life or work in this way often means that the choice of motif is conditioned more by political than artistic considerations.

Now if we transpose those ideas characteristic to the paintings of rural issues in the modern world to the context of the past hundred years of Scottish art, we should immediately grasp why the realities of Highland life have not been a crucial theme for Scottish artists. Scottish art has been unconcerned with political ideas and that rural, or even urban problems, could become part of a radical artistic cause is a concept of a role for art that has fallen on stony ground in Scotland.

Since the breakthrough of the Glasgow Boys around a century ago, the dominant subject-matter of Scottish painting has been that of landscape. Landscape became the vehicle for all progressive and experimental styles. An urban art, as had developed in France, Germany, America and England since the late nineteenth century, simply does not exist in Scotland. Neither did an art which took up the critical positions of Millet's naturalism or Courbet's realism, despite the fact that the greatest influences on Scottish painting all came from France. The Glasgow Boys adopted an open-air naturalism but were never interested in applying this to anything other than uncritical pictures of sentimental rusticity. The new methods of Cézanne and the Fauves were taken up by the Scottish Colourists, S.J. Peploe, George Leslie Hunter, and F.C.B. Cadell, who were influential between the First and Second World Wars, but again it was chiefly to landscape (including many scenes of the West Highlands) that they brought their new ideas.

After the Second World War, the mantle of Scottish modernism fell upon a group of painters who became known as the Edinburgh School. William Gillies, William McTaggart, John Maxwell, and Anne Redpath were the foremost artists of this group, and all worked or studied in France. By developing new formal and expressive approaches, they brought a clear-sighted and poetic sensibility, far removed from stereotype and kailyard sentimentality, to their view of the Scottish landscape. Their paintings, however, remain oblivious to the concrete realities of Scottish life in the mid-twentieth century.

As these artists had been instrumental in bringing certain modern ideas to Scotland they were naturally extremely influential figures and through dominating positions in art colleges and institutions such as the Royal Scottish Academy they tended to consolidate their ideas rather than open up new debates and arguments. This prevented not only a proper over-view of the diversity of the modern movement, but it also affected the way in which artists looked at all things Scottish. The act of

painting was reduced simply to the creation of a beautiful object, incapable of speaking out beyond the confines of the gallery or drawing room. There were no alternative points of view, no dissenting voices (those who disagreed were quick to leave Scotland) until the early 1960s, and only then did Scottish artists begin to think and discuss more openly and enthusiastically what art should be about. In the intervening period, to discover what life was really like in modern Scotland, we must turn to a handful of great writers.

Unlike Scottish artists, Scottish writers regard themselves as participants in a continuing struggle – a struggle for the heart, soul and future of Scotland. There is a lot at stake in Scottish literature; the field covered is rich and varied, and makes the themes explored by Scottish artists appear narrow and moribund in comparison. The wider concerns of the writers permitted rural life as a powerful source of raw material, with Highland themes forming an important part of the literary scene. With the notable exception of Hugh MacDiarmid, it could be argued that the two outstanding literary figures of the century have come from opposite sides of the Highlands, Lewis Grassic Gibbon from Aberdeenshire and Sorley MacLean from Raasay.[4]

Below: Alexander Moffatt *Sorley MacLean*. Oil on canvas, 60″ × 36″, 1978. Collection of the Scottish Arts Council

Lewis Grassic Gibbon was born James Leslie Mitchell in a croft in central Aberdeenshire in 1901. He died tragically young in 1935. Gibbon's epic trilogy, *A Scots Quair*, is about the tragic impact of civilisation on a rural community. His theme of a primitive culture being replaced by the squalor of modern life makes us aware of his links with those radical, protesting movements in modern art. It also makes us aware that more often than not, Scottish art has settled for the genteel.

Sorley MacLean was born in 1911 in Osgaig on the island of Raasay and is the first great modern Gaelic poet. MacLean's formidable achievement was to forge a new kind of Highland consciousness in his poetry, a consciousness which sprang from his personal collision at a particular historical moment (the 1930s) with the old (Gaelic culture) and the new (Communist ideology). One looks in vain for any similar cataclysmic event in modern Scottish painting.

It would be impossible to fully understand MacLean's poetry without a knowledge of Gaelic and this is admitted by the poet.[5] It would also be impossible to grasp the meaning of his poetry without some understanding of the notorious Highland Clearances. Not only have the Clearances left a bitter scar on Highland life, they have also continued to arouse deep and divisive passions throughout Scotland.

In the nineteenth century no Scottish artist set out to depict the Clearances with a view to changing social attitudes, although the subject of the Clearances did appear in the paintings of Scotland's first great modern painter, William McTaggart (1835-1910), who was the son of a crofter from Machrihanish. McTaggart passed through a Pre-Raphaelite phase to arrive at conclusions similar to those of the French Impressionists. The powerful expressive emphasis of his brush strokes coupled to textures which are clear and luminous swept away conventions of polished finish and exactitude of tedious detail. His paintings, though mainly concerned with landscape and sea-scape, include a human element, scrupulously and painstakingly placed (which suggests how important these figures were to him) within his compositions. *The Emigrants,* from the 1890s, shows evicted Highlanders about to depart for North America. He had brooded over painting an "epic of emigration" since early in his career and as a Highlander himself, he felt strongly about these paintings, feeling dissatisfied with one of the first pictures on account of its over-brightness in tone for such an unhappy event. McTaggart stands as a unique figure in Scottish art – an innovator and a Western Highlander. Unfortunately few artists were to develop the theme of forced eviction and emigration. Thomas Faed's *The Last of the Clan* compares unfavourably with McTaggart's dramatic and authentic settings. Faed remains tied to the Victorian genre of sentimental story-telling. The picture evokes pathos, but little profundity. There is, however, one exceptional painting of this period, *A Highland Funeral,* by James Guthrie (1859-1930), painted in 1882 when the artist was twenty-three years old. This starkly realistic painting shows a child's funeral in Perthshire, an event witnessed by Guthrie the year before, and implies certain affinities with Courbet's *Burial at Ornans,* although there is no real evidence of Guthrie having seen Courbet's masterpiece at that time. *A Highland Funeral* transcends the manufactured sentimentality of most paintings of Highland (and Scottish) life, expressing deeper emotions and feelings about 'ordinary folk'. Guthrie, one of the Glas-

Top: David Shanks Ewart *The Emigrants Return*. Oil on canvas, 1924. Collection of the National Galleries of Scotland
Above: John Byrne *The Cheviot, The Stag and The Black, Black Oil*. Pop-up book/stage set, 8′ × 8′, 1973. Collection of 7:84 (Scotland) Theatre Co

gow Boys, painted nothing else in this vein of Highland realism.

Few pictorial images of the Clearances feature in the twentieth century. In 1973 the 7:84 Theatre Company toured Scotland with John McGrath's *The Cheviot, The Stag and The Black, Black Oil*. McGrath's play evokes more than pity or sorrow for the Clearances by questioning the motives of those who forced the Highlanders from their homes. John Byrne's work in designing stage-sets

An image of landscape and event seen in terms of another.

Longue durée et L'histoire évenementielle.

":— those awfully picturesque ruins up on the cliffs?"

'Intimiste' conversations in a landscape of pleasure.

for 7:84 resulted in a gigantic pop-up book for "The Cheviot", which complemented the play's audacious mixture of knock-about farce and serious political comment. During the 1970s a number of artists began to re-examine the Highland landscape, discovering emotive subject-matter amongst the abandoned ruins of this disturbing environment. Frances Walker, in her closely observed drawings of deserted villages, and Reinhard Behrens (a German now domiciled in Scotland who has returned again and again to the Highlands) in his installation piece entitled *Clearances,* have both shown that this aspect of the Highlands has much to offer the contemporary artist. Simon Fraser, too, is another young artist whose visionary paintings spring from a close association with the Highlands and from "my great respect for the Gael and other indigenous cultures whose possession of archetypal marvels of wisdom is immense."[6]

A more substantial body of work taking the Clearances as its central theme was made by the Glasgow-based artist Peter Seddon in the early 1980s. In a series of large pastel drawings, Seddon utilises historical events, from both Highland history and the history of art, in order to question and challenge received historical and artistic attitudes. "Painting can be so much more than high intuitive feeling or a personal acting out of some ill-defined rage. History, for example, is a fine subject to tackle. *The Highland Clearances* series is an attempt to pay a debt to popular history, memory and cultural difference as it applies to this specific moment in Scottish history, but history in this sense different from historical spectacle or mere illustration. It is part of our cultural moment also."[7]

Perhaps the most meaningful and sustained body of work on the theme of Highland life, both past and present, by an artist living and working today is by Will MacLean. MacLean was born in Inverness in 1941, but his family roots go back to the North West coast fishing villages. He was a seaman himself before becoming an artist and his preoccupation with myth and symbol, realised not only in painting but in carved constructions and painted reliefs, owes much to a respect for the elemental spirit of the sea and its importance in the lives of fishing folk. On a personal and political level MacLean, in his work, has responded imaginatively and poetically to the Clearances and to the awful hardships endured by many Highlanders. His explorations of this

Top right: Frances Walker *Riasg Buidhe*, 1975. Watercolour and ink. Private Collection
Left: Peter Seddon (b.1947) Three works from the *Highland Clearances* series. Pastel on paper, 60″ × 60″, 1980

past have turned into elegiac icons, capable of rendering the unspeakable presence of a tormented land.

The life of a Highland crofter or fisherman depends on his own labour and that of his family. Few images of working people exist in the entire body of modern Scottish art and we may have to admit that an Englishman, Stanley Spencer, in his paintings of Clydeside shipbuilders done during the Second World War, has created the most inventive and uniquely representative images of the Scottish working-man. The outstanding visual images of Highland labour are not by a Scottish artist either, but by a Jewish artist, Josef Herman who was born in Warsaw in 1911, the son of a cobbler. Herman left Poland in 1938, and ended up in Glasgow in June 1940. Herman's painting is about the act of physical labour and survival and he has found his subjects in the Welsh mining valleys, amongst the peasants of Mexico and Spain, and in the fishing ports of the Western Highlands and the Outer Hebrides. Herman, however, is much more than an artistic tourist. "There is a tradition amongst artists, when they come to small places, to look for the so-called 'characters' and to represent them and their acts as the colour of the village. Yet a not easily satisfied observer will soon find out that the so-called 'characters' are lamentably alike everywhere. They rather remind of exotic spots on a landscape which may awaken curiosity but do not satisfy a longer interest. There is no real depth in them; and therefore they surely do not typify any place. They only have connected anecdotes, and this does not possess a big enough form to embrace a full-blooded living man, nourished by a tradition, formed by labour and moved by aspiration."[8]

Below: Will MacLean (b.1941) *Memorial to the Glendale Martyrs*. Etching, 20″ × 24″, 1983
Right: Josef Herman (b.1911) *Highland crofter*. Watercolour, 6¾″ × 9″, c1942. Collection of Robert Allison
Right top: Josef Herman *Man on tractor*. Watercolour, 8″ × 10″, c1942. Collection of Robert Allison

Herman has commented on the fact that the modern movement has ignored rural subjects, but looking at his work we can see how close he is in spirit to Millet and Van Gogh, with his concept of monumental form and his distrust of industrialisation. Although he does not show us the mechanical environment of the twentieth century, he nevertheless remains an artist for today, showing us a way of producing a human and a relevant art for our world.

Another view of Highland life is contained in a large body of work produced by James Cumming after living on Lewis for eighteen months in the early 1950s. Cumming, a distinguished and independently minded artist and an influential teacher at Edinburgh College of Art until his recent retirement, used an elaborate post-cubist style in his work at this time. This can be seen in *The Lewis Poacher*, a typical painting from his Hebridean period. Other artists such as Keith Henderson with his tautly composed painting *Wool Waulking* and Donald Smith in *The Peat Cutters* have realistically described essential moments in the working lives of the crofters, whilst Lennox Paterson takes a gentler look at the effect of civilisation on the Highland way of life in his linocut *Malcolmina is home from the City*.

All of these artists under discussion have made lasting and valuable contributions to an understanding of the realities of Highland life. In one way or another they have demolished the obvious artistic solutions to the Highland problem; that of the scenic landscape, or of the colourful 'local character'. They are in a minority of artists, not a majority, in attempting to reveal something of the historical conditions, as well as the social and political forces, which have shaped life in the Highlands over the past hundred years. Ultimately, we have to accept that the distinct cultural traditions of the Highlands have remained outwith the scope of all but a few Scottish artists. The destruction of Gaelic culture by the Clearances and the dearth of native born artists gives only a partial answer to this lamentable situation. The real reasons lie in the aloofness of the cosmopolitan artist from a depressed, and for much of the last century, a poverty-stricken society. There was nothing 'romantic' about that aspect of the Highlands: the discovery of the Highlands meant the discovery of a rare and stupendous natural environment, not the discovery of the people who lived there. This, in turn, exposes the gulf between Lowland and Highland culture. Again in turn, this leads into the confused and contradictory area of our national identity. Today, nostalgia rules in our culture and in our art and is met with little resistance. The manifestations of this nostalgia pervade everywhere throughout modern Scotland, reducing much of our cultural heritage to the pathetic level of popular kitsch. "This Scotland is not Scotland", cried MacDiarmid as he tried to shake us from our long slumber.[9]

"Other poets too, in Scotland, have seen what many have been incapable of seeing. The poets who write about the threatened societies that survive in the depopulated north and north-west, Sorley MacLean and George Mackay Brown, both refer, with an inwardness that is striking, to atomic warfare: they are like men who have already experienced some of its devastations. Few except poets have been able to see such meanings in the life of their communities. Few communities have been able to yield such meanings."[10]

The 1980s have seen the dogmas of Modernism challenged by more and more young artists like Seddon and

Above: Donald Smith (b.1926) *Men cutting peats*. Oil on board, 36″ × 24″, 1965

Donald Smith lives and works in Lewis where he was born and brought up. The cycle of croftwork and the fishing have been the central themes of his work for thirty years.

Below: James Cumming (b.1922) *The Lewis Poacher*. Oil, 19¼″ × 13″, 1954. Collection of the National Galleries of Scotland

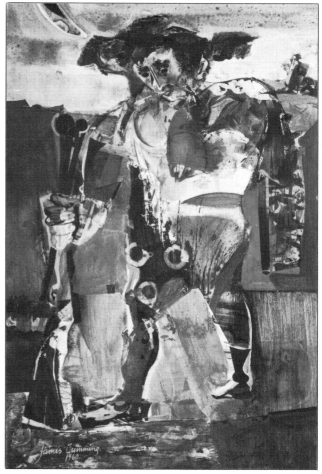

Above: Lennox Paterson (b.1915) *Malcolmina is home from the city*. Woodcut, 9″ × 6½″, 1970

MacLean. There are now new opportunities to break down the social limitations of art which seemed to be meekly accepted by earlier generations of Scottish artists. As Seddon has written, "The choice of an historical subject is not an arbitrary matter. After all, Bellini wasn't present at the crucifixion, was he?"[11] As it becomes no longer necessary to put style before content, perhaps the next generation of artists will find more in the Highlands than isolated peaks and rain-swept moors. I do not mean to despise the future potential of nature as a great subject for art. I simply wish to advance the case that there are other great subjects for artists. The poets have already shown the way.

Alexander Moffat

NOTES

1 **Wieland Schmied:** 'Points of Departure and Transformations in German Art 1905-1985'. *German Art in the 20th Century*, Royal Academy, London 1985

2 **Robert Herbert:** 'Peasant Naturalism and Millet's reputation'. *Jean-François Millet,* Arts Council of Great Britain 1976

3 As in the mural paintings of the Mexican revolution and in most forms of Third World art. Also in the post Second World War Italian cinema as in the films of Rosi, Visconti, and Bertolucci
It is interesting to note that even today the majority of the world's population consists of peasants

4 It is important to note that no great Scottish artist has been brought up in the Western Highlands in the twentieth century. Both Sorley MacLean and Iain Crichton Smith have stressed that the Fundamentalist logic of the Free Church has been in conflict with a tradition of visual imagery and poetry

5 Both MacLean and Gibbon have in their possession a weapon denied to Scottish artists. This is the linguistic power of Gaelic and Scots. For an artist to draw or paint in Gaelic or Scots is an absurd notion as the equivalent visual languages do not exist. Gibbon's aim was "to resuscitate a fully functional Scots prose that would convey the rich texture of a revitalised Scottish consciousness" (Alan Bold). Such possibilities lie outwith the available visual language(s) of painting. There are pitfalls, of course, in the use of both Gaelic and Scots – accusations of provincialism or the limitations of readership. In the cases of MacLean and Gibbon those criticisms are swept aside.

6 **Simon Fraser:** *Sireadh Bradain Sicir,* 369 Gallery, Edinburgh 1984

7 **Peter Seddon:** 'Notes on my work (*Highland Clearances*)' to the author 1986

8 **Josef Herman:** *A Welsh Mining Village.* Introduction by Jack Lindsay. Retrospective exhibition, Glasgow Art Gallery & Museum 1975

9 **Hugh MacDiarmid:** *Lament for the Great Music*, 'The Complete Poems of Hugh MacDiarmid Vol 1,' page 462 Martin, Brian and O'Keeffe, London 1978

10 **Karl Miller:** Preface, *Memoirs of a Modern Scotland,* Faber & Faber 1970

11 **Peter Seddon:** 'Notes on my work (*Highland Clearances*)'

Colour Plates: Notes

Above: *National Types*. (Left: *England*, Right: *Ireland*). Mid-19th century. Collection of Hamish MacLaren

Page 73

Full page: George Washington Wilson (1823-1893) *Corn Grinding*. Hand-coloured glass plates, 1880s. Collection of L.M.H. Smith

Washington Wilson printed his photographic images onto a 3¼ inch square glass plate, employed staff to hand-colour his work to increase its attractiveness, and sold the end product to one or more of the many lantern slide companies who, by the 1880s, were experiencing an unprecedented demand for new and interesting material. The images could be magnified in excess of five thousand times to produce a picture twenty feet square. The Washington Wilson photographs reproduced in *From the Land* have been selected from a series recently discovered in the basement of a Lancashire mill which was about to be demolished. The slides date from the 1880s and were the product of several visits which Washington Wilson, as Photographer Royal for Scotland, made to the Highlands and Islands.

Corn Grinding

The lecture notes accompanying this lantern slide of Skye in the 1880s read: "This is a very old custom still existing in Skye. The quantity of oats raised by a crofter in a good season is not large, and not infrequently, as the result of an unfavourable season, or the ravages of deer, it is too insignificant to take to the mill. In such a case the 'clach-cuaich' is brought into requisition. (As shown by the woman) . . . In order to remove the outer husk it is then sifted through a sieve, made by stretching a sheepskin on a frame and then perforating it all over with a red hot iron. The old man in the picture holds a sieve of this description.

An old law from so far back as the thirteenth century provided that no man shall presume to grind his own grain excepting in very peculiar circumstances. More recently the laird could oblige his tenants to make use of the more expeditious methods of grinding and empowered his miller "to search out and break any querns he can find" as machines that defraud him of the toll."

Page 74

Top: George Washington Wilson (1823-1893) *Loch Boisdale, South Uist*. Hand-coloured glass plate, 1880s. Collection of L.M.H. Smith

The lecture notes accompanying this lantern slide read: "Besides kelp making, at which old and young join, there is lobster fishing and Loch Boisdale is often the scene of all the hustle and excitement accompanying a good herring season".

Bottom: George Washington Wilson (1823-1893) *St Kilda Parliament*. Hand-coloured glass plate, 1880s. Collection of L.M.H. Smith

The lecture notes accompanying this, now famous, lantern slide read: "Beyond the reach of the laws that govern this realm they make their own laws. The solitary minister on the island may advise on certain matters, and certainly has a limited influence, but it is their Parliament that fixes matters beyond appeal, and no stranger may take part in its deliberations.

This Parliament meets daily, discusses the weather and state of the sea etc. in a few Gaelic phrases; and by a majority the order of the day is fixed, and no single individual takes it upon himself to arrange his own business until after they unitedly decide what is best".

Page 75

Top right: H.J. Dobson *The Crofter's Grace*. 'Scottish Life and Character' Series II. Raphael Tuck and Sons. Scotch Myths Archive

Bottom: Edwin Landseer (1803-1873) *Monarch of the Glen*. Oil on canvas, 64½" × 66½". Collection of John Dewar and Son

The most famous image of the Highlands was originally intended for the refreshment rooms of the House of Lords. It perfectly expresses the Victorian ideal of the Highlands as untamed wilderness, albeit man-made wilderness.

The original of the "Stag at bay/Lord of all I survey" gentre.

Page 76

National Types

Top left: Poster for the film production *Scotch Myths*, written and directed by Murray Grigor, and produced by Barbara Grigor. Scotch Myths Archive

Bottom left: *The Cock o' the North*. 'Highland Laddies' Series, Raphael Tuck and Sons. Scotch Myths Archive

Top right: *Wha's Like Us?* 'National Series' postcard, Miller and Lang. Scotch Myths Archive

Bottom right: *The Scotsman*. 'National Types'. Collection of Hamish MacLaren

While every nation may be said to have its 'national type', the caricature of the 'Hielander' is simultaneously one of the most developed and the most grotesque.

"Those who cannot be subdued into conforming to the British norm are ridiculed, and truth is exaggerated to the level of parody and travesty. The received image is then accepted as 'the way they are'." Frank Thompson.

The postcards reproduced in the Colour Section, and generally throughout the book in black and white, are from the Scotch Myths Archive. The pioneering exhibition *Scotch Myths – an Exploration of Scotchness*, which considered the vexed question of Scottish National identity, was organised by Murray and Barbara Grigor, who stated "Our principal aim is to question a culture that continues to portray itself in distorted national stereotypes".

Page 77

Highland 'Kailyard'

Top right: *A Highland Washing*. 'Artotype Series', Valentine and Sons Ltd. Scotch Myths Archive

Middle right: *Give us a bit of your kilt laddie*. 'Burlesque Series No. 101', Eustace Watkins. Scotch Myths Archive

Bottom right: *Bonnie Scotland*. 'Highland Laddies' Series, Raphael Tuck and Sons. Scotch Myths Archive

By the end of the 19th and the beginning of the 20th centuries the postcard industry was booming, and 'Scotchness' offered a rich vein of humour and sentiment, as well as romance.

The Highland 'Kailyard' genre illustrated by the three images on this page condescendingly substitutes tamed, tartanned and puritanical parochiality for the glamorous myth of the Romantic Highlands.

The image (top) of Highland women trampling washing with hitched skirts was one of the most outstandingly successful postcard themes and numerous variations exist. The sight of female ankles, and a glimpse of thigh, were considered so unusual by the Victorian and Edwardian public that these ostensibly inoffensive postcards were extremely risqué for their time.

Above: George Washington Wilson (1823-1893) *Corn Grinding*. Hand-coloured glass plate, 1880s. Collection of L.M.H. Smith

Above: George Washington Wilson (1823-1893) *Loch Boisdale, South Uist.* Hand-coloured glass plate, 1880s. Collection of L.M.H. Smith

Below: George Washington Wilson (1823-1893) *St Kilda Parliament.* Hand-coloured glass plate, 1880s. Collection of L.M.H. Smith

THE CROFTER'S GRACE.

Right: H.J. Dobson *The Crofter's Grace*. 'Scottish Life and Character' Series II. Raphael Tuck and Sons. Scotch Myths Archive

Below: Edwin Landseer (1803-1873) *Monarch of the Glen*. Oil on canvas, 64½″ × 66½″. Collection of John Dewar and Son

SCOTCH
MYTHS
an exploration of scotchness

JOHN BETT   FREDDIE BOARDLEY   JULIET CADZOW   WALTER CARR
ROBBIE COLTRANE   SAMUEL FULLER   RON GEESIN
SOREL JOHNSON   CHIC MURRAY   ALEX NORTON   BILL PATERSON
BRIAN PETTIFER   DAVID RINTOUL   FINLAY WELSH

PHOTOGRAPHY: MARK LITTLEWOOD   EDITOR: PATRICK HIGSON
MUSIC: RON GEESIN   ANIMATION: DONALD HOLWILL
PRODUCER: BARBARA GRIGOR   WRITTEN & DIRECTED BY MURRAY GRIGOR

Far left: Poster for the film *Scotch Myths*, written and directed by Murray Grigor, and produced by Barbara Grigor. Scotch Myths Archive

Left: *Wha's Like Us?* 'National Series' postcard, Miller and Lang. Scotch Myths Archive

Right: *A Highland Washing*. 'Artotype Series', Valentine and Sons Ltd. Scotch Myths Archive

Right: *Give us a bit of your kilt laddie*. 'Burlesque Series No. 101', Eustace Watkins. Scotch Myths Archive

Far left: *The Cock o'the North*. 'Highland Laddies' Series, Raphael Tuck and Sons. Scotch Myths Archive

Left: *The Scotsman*. 'National Types'. Collection of Hamish MacLaren

Right: *Bonnie Scotland*. 'Highland Laddies' Series, Raphael Tuck and Sons. Scotch Myths Archive

KING GEORGE V.

WHEN THE KILTY LADS COME HOME (1).

In an old-fashion'd cottage, in yon Highland glen,
Sits a loving Scotch mother, nigh threescore and ten ;
Her four sons are fighting for Freedom and Right,
And the mother sings proudly from morning till night

"ONY MAIR
TAE SLEW?"

("Am bheil tuilleadh
ri mharbhadh?")

THE PUIR WEE GAIRMAN LADDIE!

Above: *Milking Time*. 'In the Highlands' Series, Ralph Tuck and Sons. Scotch Myths Archive

Below: Manfred Bluth *Die Frierender Schafe* (The Freezing Sheep). Oil on canvas, 44″ × 48″, 1979

Above: William McTaggart (1835-1910) *Crofter Emigrants Leaving the Hebrides*. Oil on canvas, 57″ × 85″, 1891
Collection of Kirkcaldy Art Gallery and Museum

Below: Keith Henderson (1883-1982) *Wool Waulking*. Oil on canvas, 40″ × 60″, 1927-28
Collection of the School of Scottish Studies, Edinburgh University

Top: Peter Seddon (b.1947) *The Highland Clearances Series:
"Memories construct a different picture"*. Pastel on paper, 60″ ×
60″, 1980
Left: Will MacLean (b.1941) *Memorial for a Clearance Village*.
Mixed media construction, 16″ × 23″ × 3″, 1976. Collection of
Mrs F. Sutherland
Below: Neil MacPherson (b.1954) *Singing Shepherd*. Acrylic and
collage, 45″ × 52″, 1985

Above: Will MacLean *Sabbath of the Dead*. Mixed media construction, 15″ × 27″ × 4″, 1978.
Private Collection

Below: Reinhard Behrens (b.1951) *Clearances*. Oil, driftwood, found shoes, 152″ × 62″, 1984

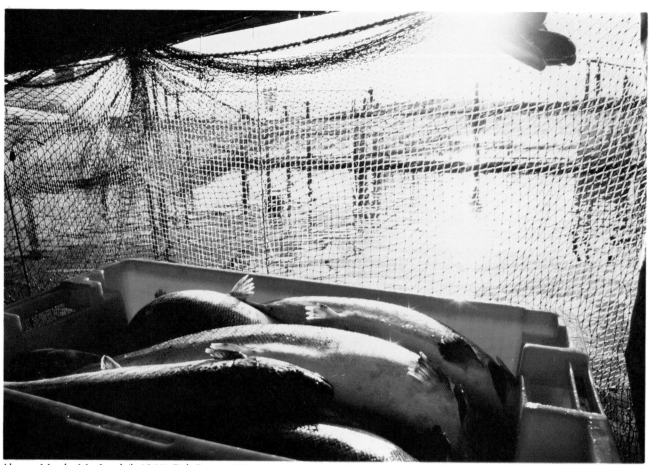

Above: Murdo MacLeod (b.1964) *Fish Farm*, 1986

Below: Murdo MacLeod *Reagan at Callanish*, 1986

Page 78

Patriotism and War

Top left: *H.M. King George V.* Raphael Tuck and Sons. Scotch Myths Archive

Bottom left: *Ony Mair Tae Slew.* 'National Series', Millar and Lang. Scotch Myths Archive

Top right: *When the Kilty Lads Come Home.* 'Song' series, Bamforth and Co. Ltd. Scottish Myths Archive. *The Puir Wee Gairman Laddie!* Publisher unknown. Scotch Myths Archive

The fighting prowess of the Highlander has always been exploited for British glory. "No great mischief if they fall," stated General Wolfe, who advocated the recruitment of Highlanders for British military service

Page 79

Top right: *Dunrobin Castle.* 'Scottish Clans' Series VI, Raphael Tuck and Sons. Scotch Myths Archive

Middle right: *Dear Fr-reend.* 'Scotch Message' Postcards, Valentine and Sons Ltd. Scotch Myths Archive

Bottom right: *The Land for the People.* Cynicus Art Publishing Co. Scotch Myths Archive

By wrapping Dunrobin Castle in cosy Tartanry, it ceases to be a symbol of absolute power and repression (unmatched in recent British history), and becomes something altogether more homely and 'traditional'.

'Cynicus' presents the alternative version of Highland reality which contrasts strongly with both Dunrobin Castle and the ludicrous 'music hall' sentimentality of the postcard in between.

Page 80

Top: *Milking Time,* 'In the Highlands' Series, Ralph Tuck and Sons. Scotch Myths Archive

Bottom: Manfred Bluth *Die Frierender Schafe* (The Freezing Sheep). Oil on canvas, 44″ × 48″, 1979

"I have to state that we poor people have been sent to a headland of the sea where it was not worth-while to send sheep forty years ago, and that was the reason we were sent there. We were crowded altogether upon it . . . Many of these were sent from the other townships that were cleared – poor people that could not go away to America. Because there was no other place for them, they were hurled in upon that headland. When I open my door there is no place within the range of my sight except where there are big sheep . . ."

Alexander MacDonald of Crowlista, giving evidence to the Napier Commission, 1883.

Page 81

Top: William McTaggart *Crofter Emigrants Leaving the Hebrides.* Oil on canvas, 57″ × 85″, 1891. Collection of Kirkcaldy Art Gallery and Museum

This painting is one of a series on the theme of Highland emigration by McTaggart, who was one of the most innovative and successful Scottish artists. He came from a West Highland crofting background and had brooded about painting an "epic of emigration" since early in his career.

Bottom: Keith Henderson (1883-1982) *Wool Waulking.* Oil on canvas, 40″ × 60″, 1927-28. Collection of the School of Scottish Studies, Edinburgh University

In *Gaelic Folksongs from the Isle of Barra,* Annie Johnston describes the wool waulking and the rich repertoire of associated songs known as "Orin Luaidh".

"The number of waulking women was according to the size of the cloth, and if it was blue cloth, there had to be two teams, working in turn, to make it really tight. Usually five or six was the number that could sit on each side of the waulking-board. The women used to come, wearing calico petticoats, drugget coats and tibbet aprons. Then the hostess used to baptize the cloth, that is, she shook holy water on it in the name of the Trinity, and put it in a tub of urine. They used to say that nothing was so good for taking the oil out (of the cloth) as urine. They used to take the cloth out of the tub and put it on the board, as you saw, and doubled it on the board

thus. Then the woman who was best at singing began with a slow song to encourage them because they were getting tired.

After this the hostess would measure the cloth with her middle finger, and usually there was not much shrinking in it at the first three songs. Then another one would begin; she would sing three songs too, and as the cloth had been warmed by the first three songs, it would shrink more at the second attempt, and at the third attempt it ought to be ready, if it were a blanket or white cloth."

It was considered unlucky for the same song to be sung twice at a waulking.

Page 82

Top right: Peter Seddon (b.1947) *The Highland Clearances Series; "Memories construct a different picture".* Pastel on paper, 60″ × 60″, 1980

Peter Seddon's large pastel series uses a range of visual references (from art history and other disciplines) to locate the Clearances in a wider context and create a variety of fresh associations.

Top left: Will MacLean (b.1941, Inverness) *Memorial for a Clearance Village.* Mixed media construction, 16″ × 23″ × 3″, 1976. Collection of Mrs F. Sutherland

The Clearances and their consequences have been a recurrent subject in Will MacLean's work for many years. His mixed media constructions represent the single most consistent and significant body of contemporary art work on the theme of Highland history.

Bottom: Neil MacPherson (b.1954) *Singing Shepherd.* Acrylic and collage, 45″ × 52″, 1985

Page 83

Top: Will MacLean (b.1941) *Sabbath of the Dead.* Mixed media construction, 15″ × 27″ × 4″, 1978. Private Collection

Bottom: Reinhard Behrens (b.1951). *Clearances.* Oil, driftwood, found shoes, 152″ × 62″, 1984

Have the people of the Island made any formal application to the proprietor or his factor in reference to this overcrowding?
We spoke of it several times to the factor and the reply we got was to go to America.
Norman MacDonald of Scarp, Harris, giving evidence to the Napier Commission

Page 84

Top: Murdo MacLeod (b.1964, Shawbost, Lewis) *Fish Farm.* Photograph, 1986

Bottom: Murdo MacLeod *Reagan at Callanish.* Photograph, 1986

Murdo MacLeod has rapidly established himself as one of Scotland's foremost photographers. As a young Gael his images of Highland life are sympathetic but unclouded by false sentiment.

Below: Maxie Bain *Neil Gunn* (1891-1972). Collection of the Scottish Arts Council

85

"Have you got your luggage all richt, Wullie?"

"Weel, I dunno, I micht have to buy anither bottle when I reach Glasga!"

Above: Published by Bamforth and Co. Ltd. Scotch Myths Archive

Below: Tonal' (to English tourist): *"I doot we're gaun ta hae a shoo'r."* Published by Valentine and Sons Ltd. Postmark, 1903. Scotch Myths Archive

KIND, KIND AND GENTLE IS SHE.

Above: *Kind, kind and gentle is she*. Postmark, 1908. Scotch Myths Archive

Valentine's   Tonal (to English tourist): "I doot we're gaun ta hae a shoo'r."   Series 158

Whistlers in the Dark:
The Hielan Picture Postcard

Please consider the entries described below for inclusion in a possible exhibition.

1   Churchyard in the Scottish Highlands . . . As a result of an altercation in an inn earlier that day, three ministers — Thomas, William and Charles Pape — confront three local anti-heroes, John and Hucheon MacPhail and William Murray. An armed brawl begins. Charles Pape wounds William Murray in the face and Murray kills him.
(This sequence comes from a silent Gaelic documentary made in Dornoch, Sutherland in 1607.)

2   A late nineteenth century cartoon in the *Punch* style . . . a domestic interior in the village of Barvas, Isle of Lewis, with figures and this caption: "Sad as were the scenes I had visited on the previous two days, they were not so heartrending as the sight which presented itself to me on entering the miserable bothy occupied by John Murray. There was as usual the manure heap, and around the fire on straw pallets four sick children were lying, their wan, pinched faces telling only too plainly the story of want and poverty . . ."

3   An early twentieth century postcard . . . on the front, a photograph entitled "Parliament Building from the East, Ottawa, Canada" . . . on the back, a message handwritten in indelible pencil:

> Dear Parents
> I hope this will
> find you all well.
> The rest of my Bros
> is in the best of
> spirits I will
> write you soon
> wishing this will
> find you all well. Neil

The card is addressed to Mr John Murray in Barvas — John of the miserable bothy, descendant of William, the seventeenth century fugitive from Sutherland.
(Neil was killed in action in France in the 1914-18 war.)

How many maudlin songs, lugubrious quatrains, stereotype images could be prompted be these three snapshots?

John Murray, descendant of William the blacksmith, was my grandfather; my name is his as it was his grandfather's before him. I grew up on the croft in Barvas. I remember very well the extent to which this windswept township wound itself in tartan and conducted its daily life like an untidy operetta, endless lilting and sycophantically skippily heel-and-toeing, pausing only to have drops of the cratur or to complete application forms for social security subsidy . . . while, in the heather-purple lochan, the royal stag's legs dissolved as it tried to conjure up a title for a painting of the Monarch and John Brown, whose kilt goes gloaming on . . .

Had the Highland Temperance League been founded three centuries earlier, life might have been very different for William Murray and death for Charles Pape. Murray could have continued his work as a bow-maker in Sutherland — founded a multi-national armaments company — instead of becoming a blacksmith in Lewis. Had he been fortunate enough to be familiar with the ancient (mid-nineteenth century) rules governing his particular clan, he would have known that his crest was "a demi-savage, proper, holding in his right hand a dagger, proper, pommel and hilt, or, and in his left hand a key, or". Had he known how proper clansfolk dressed, he would have realised how inappropriate it was to brandish a sword while in every day clothing: "a sword is worn with court dress and the wearing of a dirk may have some justification . . ." And, hoots mon, hoch-och, it was evening and "for evening wear, sporrans made of baby seal or other light coloured skins are worn . . ."

Similarly, Mrs Murray of the nineteenth century, knowing that a visitor was approaching, ought to have hitched up her skirt and put on an impromptu blanket-trampling display, or at least sung songs about the Kilty Lads freedom-fighting in the South African wars — or even "Granny's Hielan Hame". In this century, had Neil not been beguiled by the cachet of Princess Pat's Canadian Light Infantry, he might have survived to post his own postcards and to get walk-on parts in Hollywood Highland movies. Incidentally, it is likely that he would have noticed in the course of various big 'pushes' in France how desperate the Germans were to shoot Highlanders, just to find out what they wore under their kilts. (Achtung! Ma conscience!)

Some cartoon, film and postcard drawings of Highland people are sexually significant. Prurience probably caused a rash of portrayals of bare-thighed women standing fetchingly in tubs, and who dares guess what subconscious hang-ups gave rise to the under-the-kilt

Below: *Parliament Building from the East* . . . (see above).
Right: Reverse side. Collection of John Murray

theme? Generally, however, the Highlander is not depicted as a sex symbol and remains more oatcake than cheesecake. Most frequently, males and females appear as dummies in speckled drapery to which bits of flora and fauna have been stuck. Quite often, too, the people portrayed seem to have escaped from the murkier sections of nineteenth century illustrated medical dictionaries. Men always clasp something — usually bottles — to assuage the lingering pain of having their swords, pommels and hilt an' a', removed.

Highlanders, as they emerge from this welter of popular images, seem to have all the sartorial, physical, emotional and intellectual qualities (and the oomph) of garden gnomes. They also match the garden gnome in unimportance. The male mac-gnome may wear a jovial or furious expression, the female may hold her leg in the air in mid-pas-de-bas, or whatever other model attitude takes your fancy in the Gaelic Garden Gnomemporium, but it is of no consequence, merely a useful conversation piece. After all, you bought it and when its novelty palls, you can either shift it to some other corner of the garden or discard it and buy into another more fashionable minority. This way, you cheat the thistle and get only the 'silk' from life.

Ah yes, it is easy to build up a head of steam, to vital-spark off a fiery-cross rage, to invoke four-pronged curses on the progeny of the hacks who produced some of the popular images; it might balance all the ancient and abiding wrongs perpetrated upon us by somebody out there (ochone a-ri-ri oro). But haud yer horses an' dinna fash yersel ower much. Did not some of ourselves scrabble our way outwards and ever upwards to gain a foothold in the cumulo-nimbus of the lower middle classes? And did not an occasional MacSomeone make it to the Top, shedding kilt and pipes and parents and language en route — all but the sporran? ("Sporrans made of animal skins with hair too long detract from the dignity of the kilt.") Did not Sir John Alexander MacDonald, son of Highlanders cleared from Sutherland, become the first Prime Minister of Canada in 1867 . . . Was not his chief opponent Alexander Mackenzie from Perthshire, who ousted MacDonald in 1873 for a few years . . . Wha, indeed, is like us? And when as a result of Clearances in the United States, a band of Sioux led by Tatanka Yotanka (Sitting Bull) crossed into Canada for refuge, how were they treated by the Canadian Highlanders?

Consider the following as an alternative caption for the Neil Murray postcard showing "Parliament Building from the East, Ottawa, Canada":

Sir John MacDonald:
I do not see how a Sitting Bull
can cross the frontier.
Mr Mackenzie:
Not unless he rises.
Sir John MacDonald:
Then he is not a Sitting Bull.

[Canada House of Commons Debate, 1878]

Much too easy to indulge in fury — and there's a risk of self-injury.

In the blank spaces provided below, please insert the word "not" as you see fit. Winners will receive an engraved musical haggis.

Of course, we are .... barbaric, mean, sanctimonious chanters of interminable songs about funerals, who spend the winter slaughtering livestock to

FOU THE NOO.

Above: *The National Series*. Postmark, 1904. Scotch Myths Archive

Below: Postcard. Scotch Myths Archive

NOO, SINGLE MEN, JUST TAK' MY TIP, AN' BE A
  WEE BIT FLY,
AYE WATCH THE HIELAN' MARYS THAT
WERE NEVER BORN IN SKYE.

STANDING ON HIS DIGNITY

Shipping Agent. "Are you a mechanic?"
Intending Emigrant (justly indignant). "*No!*—I'm a Macpherson!"

Above: *Punch* Magazine

Up to the turn of the century 75% of the unsolicited jokes printed in Punch *came from Scotland*

Below: *Punch* Magazine

Q. E. D.

Professor McPhairrson. "No, Mrs. Brown, it's not that we Scots are dull; but you English see a joke in *anything*! Why, the other day I was in a room with four Englishmen, one of whom told a story, and, would you believe it, I was the only man that didn't laugh!"

make bagpipes. Of course, we are .... the last remnants of a noble, brave, generous race who conquered Europe, lovers of poetry and music. We are .... a thick red line, a ferocious skirted army gloriously dying at ramparts everywhere. We are- .... cunning peasants who eat all protected species of wildlife, non-viable and scenically disastrous. We are .... homo mac-alastair-pithecus, a walking Glencoe, articulating porridge and eructating pibroch. We are .... the flooers o' the forest, humble, humorous and engagingly independent.

Much too easy to swap slogan for slogan. Like company logos, they satisfy the desire for simultaneous camouflage and exposure, that's all.

Neil Murray, son of John, lived and emigrated, like four of his brothers, to Canada. But if you could see only the face of the postcard he sent you would know nothing about Neil. The message on the front bears no relation to the message on the back. Neil, like all ordinary Highlanders then and now, lived and died on the dark side of the postcard, not on its public face.

Although the making of these postcard images is based on some kind of 'documentary' approach, it does not deal with the reality of people's experience or surroundings: indeed, it avoids that — deliberately? (Aye — weel . . .) So the humour does not spring from the people portrayed. Where, then, does it come from? A joke-box?

These images do, however, define very clearly for the parties involved whose side they're on in the prevailing current opinion.

The portrayer's stance is the power-base of contemporary social and economic attitudes; the subject — the victim — looking down the wrong end of the barrel of brush or lens, has no stance. He just knows he's not the artist. It is also clear that the 'artist' does not in the slightest identify or even sympathise with his subject, choosing instead to use the latter to reinforce for himself and his peers their belief that they are not the lowest social order, nor even so low as to be the butt of jokes . . .

Ach, but we wass after thinking (hic!) can you not take a joke, mac? What harm can there be in one humorous postcard, one film, one novel, one song or, indeed, in one rem of radioactivity? None, of course. Unless it is mass-produced and distributed all over the world to people who don't know it is meant to be a family joke, who have no other truer image to measure it against. Then the popular perception of Highlanders is based upon such images alone . . . Thus doth propagation produce propaganda.

In the north of Scotland many centuries ago, people built high, commodious, circular stone forts, probably as refuges for themselves and their goods and chattels in times of trouble (Yon awfa' savage Vikings wi' the horns, ye ken . . .) A number of these forts were built on islets in the middle of lochs, connected to the shore by submerged stone causeways. Some of these causeways had sudden sharp bends or irregularities, some had occasional wobbly flagstones which drummed out a very loud warning of one's approach. Some causeways had more than one of these traps — it depended, not upon the bravery or prestige of the builders, but upon the wit of the artist who designed the pathway.

Wit is not ephemeral. Wit will develop and ignite only when a creative imagination is engaged with the world about it. (Whit?) There is no such thing as corporate wit

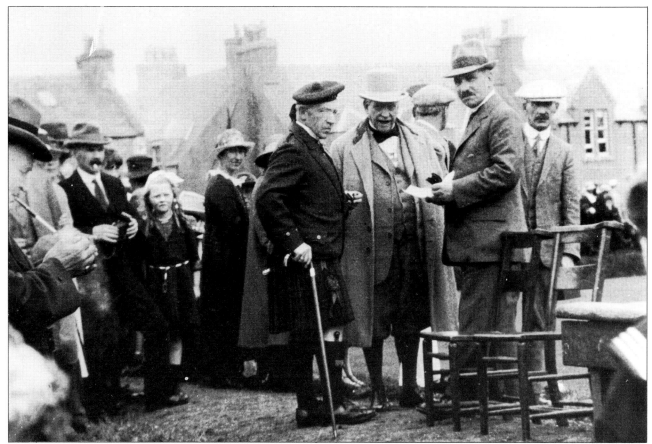

Above: *Sir Harry Lauder and Lord Leverhulme, proprietor of Lewis and Harris, in Stornoway, 1920.* Collection of Deirdre MacDonald

"*Broadway 1907. New York, New York. The curtain rises on the twentieth century revealing a painted backcloth. A stag at bay. The fairyland palace of Balmoral. To the strains of* Roaming in the Gloaming *in tramps a wee kilted mannie in blue bonnet and bow tie. The Scotch comic has arrived with a drink in one hand and a claymore in the other.*"
                                                              Brian Dunnigan

— say, displayed by the World Oilco Inc., or the Union of Floor, Ceiling and Plate Polishers: wit is an attribute of individuals only.

Almost all popular portrayals of Highlanders are humorous, or at least 'good-humoured' and are founded on the belief that to laugh and almost cry simultaneously is the acme of experience for the target audience (and for the simple, pawky Highlander). Over the years, several cliches have been cast, a rigid framework of reference has been forged. The range of emotional response is severely limited:-

> pride + optional single tear + laughter
> pride + single tear + smile
> pride + thousand tears + smiling through
> pride + thousand tears + optional faint smile for posterity

The absence of any individual track left by the artist, the general lack of imagination, wit, or creativity and the shallow formulaic approach separate such works from the reality of life in the Highlands.

Yet they exist and it is very interesting indeed to have such a collection in this context. Normally, we see only single items. A collection of this scale allows us to discern characteristics, to note any trends or lines of development. Is there any development in this genre? I do not believe there is, other than that which results from advancing technology: the images can be reproduced more quickly or in greater minute variety or more picturesquely, but the thematic range remains the same. A moderately-clever computer-graphics programme linked to an analysis of scanty emotional range could do wonders for this trade. This kind of material runs along tracks as predictable as railway lines (no-one need fall into the loch when approaching the fortress from which this material comes). Because of the remoteness from external reality, later pictures can only grow from earlier pictures, so the overall effect is as annoying and unenlightening as an ingrowing toenail.

Let's go back to the beginning. Consider another entry for yonder possible exhibition:

Velvet, palpably black November night, west coast of Lewis in the 1950s. A boy is walking home alone, clomping his boots on tarmac to check he is still on the road . . . in his head, a burning bright tiger rises behind him and almost silently pads along after him, gathering its muscles for the spring. Summoning all his evaporating courage, the boy begins to whistle a tune loudly — "All the blue bonnets are over the border." The tiger, perplexed, fades and the boy runs home like lightning . . . (wha' daur meddle wi' me?)

[I was that boy, and whistled much in winter.]

Around the dark edges of civilised consciousness pads a shadowy, silent watcher, generating aboriginality. A stalker who must be kept beyond the pale, as inappropriate in an orderly, sophisticated head as Blake's tiger in Barvas. There is a strain of visual art which will never confront that stalking figure, but will instead search the daylit world for a tame surrogate whipping-boy. It may be that, for a considerable period, the Highlander has fulfilled that role (as have many other minority cultures) for more powerful neighbours.

Above: *Poor Jock*. Scotch Myths Archive

Above: *We are Not Downhearted at Mallaig.* "Mailing Novelty" Published by Valentine and Sons Ltd. Scotch Myths Archive

But these images are popular and Highlanders like them too, don't they? There is so much of the stuff . . . It has been distributed so widely for so many generations that descendants of Highlanders in other countries hang their Scottish Highland identity on the peg it provides. Not only descendants of Highland exiles are affected. Gradually, the material and the perception of us it represents filters its way back and is absorbed into our lives, eventually being proudly possessed by us, traditionalised, believed.

And, help-ma-boab, we ourselves begin to enact the travesty. We add to the corpus of wee bens, wee grannies, wee churches, wee bottles, insisting that our own wee home-grown ethnicised material is better than any imports. We massage ourselves and those who mock us. It is puzzling . . . For some reason the Highlander has not developed a strong tradition of native visual art, and that is unfortunate for us. There could be no surer defence against the kind of visual representation exemplified here than that it could be measured against our own range of images of ourselves, but we remain content to inhabit only the backs of postcards.

Regardless of our own inabilities, however, it is quite clear that these portrayals of our race are not informed by understanding, not illuminated by wit or sympathy and that they denigrate and ridicule us, for no apparent reason. So, with some reluctance, I conclude that this part of the exhibition, including the best-kept images of the Highlander, is undoubtedly not art, and that the images in it are symptoms of the plague of racism.

Please read and sign the following declaration (Highlanders are not excluded from this instruction):

> I promise by Divine assistance to
> abstain from RACIST PORTRAYALS
> and to discountenance all the causes
> and practices of SUCH INTOLERANCE

Signed................................ Date ....

wishing this will
find you all well. John Murray.

John Murray

Below: *Highland Temperance League Certificate*, 1883. Collection of the People's Palace Museum, Glasgow

Above: *Piper Kenneth MacKay of the 79th Cameron Highlanders at the Battle of Waterloo, 1815*. (From a painting by Lockhart Bogle.)

The Highland Regiments became an important fighting force within the British Army and participated in virtually all the British Empire's theatres of war. Collection of Queen's Own Highlanders

Below: *The military tradition ensured that the Highland Regiments featured prominently in the bloodbath of the First World War, which decimated the male population of many Highland villages.*

Above: *Lewismen of the Seaforth Highlanders in France, 1915. Studio Portrait.* Courtesy of Roderick MacLean

The Armed Forces

Far right: Sam Maynard *Nato Base, Stornoway, 1985*

Since the 1950s the West Highlands have become one of the most densely militarised areas of Europe with rocket ranges in the Uists, radar stations on St Kilda, torpedo testing grounds around Skye and a controversial Nato Base imposed upon Stornoway against the wishes of the Western Isles Council.

Above: *The mast of the* SS Iolaire. *The* Iolaire *sank at the entrance to Stornoway harbour early on New Year's morning, 1919. Nearly two hundred returning servicemen drowned within sight of Stornoway quay.* Collection of Mrs. James MacLean

Below: *Lewis Sailors. The seafaring tradition in the West Highlands has a long history. These young Lewis sailors sat for this studio photograph in Portsmouth during the First World War.* Collection of Roderick Murray

Above: Dan Morrison *Gathered round in the evening for a drink in the old* Eoropie *bothan*, 1950s

The illegal bothans, or informal drinking clubs, were well known in rural Lewis and subject to only occasional raids by the police.

Drink

Below: Sam Maynard *"Zebos", Stornoway*, 1986

Glossy, disco décor is now more commonplace in Island pubs than the informality of the bothan

Top right: *Angus Og. He quotes here from the police evidence to the court following one particularly memorable* bothan *raid*

Near right: John Pettie (1839-1893) *Tussle with a Highland Smuggler*. Oil on canvas, 1868. Collection of Aberdeen Art Gallery

The Highlander as demonic savage in conflict with the forces of law and order, personified in the stout and resolute figure of the exciseman.

Middle far right: *Punch* Magazine

Bottom far right: *Faither must be hame*. Scotch Myths Archive

Bottom right: *Punch* Magazine

JUDGING BY APPEARANCES

Old Scots Wife. "Losh me ! There's a maun drenkin' oot o' twa boattles at ance !!"

[*The old gentleman was trying his new binocular, a Christmas present to his nephew.*]

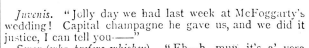

Juvenis. "Jolly day we had last week at McFoggarty's wedding ! Capital champagne he gave us, and we did it justice, I can tell you——"

Senex (who prefers whiskey). "Eh—h, mun, it's a' vera weel weddings at ye-er time o' life. Gie me a gude solid funeral !"

Above: Gus Wylie *Schoolroom in Vatersay, 1970s*
Vatersay, off Barra, is predominantly a Roman Catholic island.

Religion

Left: Minister: *"Don't you know, Johnnie, that it's wrong to catch fish on the Sabbath?"*
Johnnie: *"Wha's catchin' fush?"*
Valentine and Sons Ltd. Scotch Myths Archive

Below: *The Church.* Scotch Myths Archive
The Kirk has long been a favourite butt of the cartoonist. When the Free Church combined with the United Presbyterians in 1900 to form the United Free Church, it triggered a dispute which became the subject of a postcard series. Twenty-six Free Church ministers refused to enter the new denomination and subsequently gained control of the old Free Church's financial assets.

Above: Murdo MacLeod *Family worship, Lewis,* 1986

"Lewis is predominantly Presbyterian, and in the morning and in the evening families will sit down, in working clothes, to read some scripture and a psalm. Far away from the quiet lament beside them the children watch the adults' furrowed brows and grey hairs and dream of games, shore, moor, television, boats and discos."

Murdo MacLeod

Below: Sam Maynard *The Reverend Angus Smith, Moderator of the Free Church of Scotland,* 1986

The Reverend Smith is a controversial figure who was arrested for obstructing the first Sunday ferry to land on Skye. A religious fundamentalist, he has come to represent the ultra-conservatism that many now associate with the Free Church.

Above: *Brigadoon*, 1954. Collection of the B.F.I.
Below: *Whisky Galore*, 1948. American title, *Tight Little Island*.
Collection of the British Film Institute (B.F.I.)

The Moving Picture

The first image I ever saw was that of a red speckled hen pecking at some wispy straw. It was brought to us courtesy of Cailleach nan Cearcan ("The Poultry Lady") who toured the Western Isles in the late fifties with a slide show aimed at converting the crofters to the wonders of poultry production.

It was, I suppose, an inauspicious introduction to the glittering world of images. My one consolation may be that the red speckled hen and the other forgotten images of that evening of a quarter of a century ago were at least ethnic and authentic.

At about the same time less ethnic but more memorable images arrived in Uist. These were the real 'Pictures' which began to be shown each Saturday night in the church hall at Daliburgh courtesy of the Highlands and Islands Film Guild.

I particularly remember setting off one fading Autumn evening to walk the eight miles to the church hall to watch the latest adventures of Roy Rogers. Half a mile from our home I was given a lift in Domhnall Nellie's car and as we drove along the bumpy road he switched on the car wireless – the first time I'd ever seen or heard such a phenomenon. I remember that Radio Luxembourg was playing, and I became so absorbed by the music emerging from the wavering red dial that I have forgotten the no doubt wonderful Hollywood images of later that evening. That incident serves to remind us that, in the right circumstances, radio can be much more powerful and memorable than film or television.

At school also the memorable images were those associated with that which was strange and distant. We read story books on Friday afternoons and as the schoolmaster dozed and smoked his brier pipe we formed images of places and wonders far removed from Garrynamonie: *Treasure Island, Coral Island, Black Beauty*. All the books told of distant lands and great adventures, and all of them – with the exception of one – were in English.

The exception was *Laithean Geala* by Murchadh MacLeoid. But even that title sounded wonderfully romantic to us – *White Days* – and inside, it told happy tales of sun-soaked days on the shieling in Lewis: secure images which seemed to contrast somewhat sharply with the constant rain and frequent disappointment that seemed to beset us in Uist. This place where boys played in blue rocky pools and lambs gambolled in the white cotton grass became as wonderful to us as *Treasure Island* itself, and because of *Laithean Geala* I had, until my late teens, an image of Lewis as a far-off sun-soaked island where boys and girls and collie dogs played on the shieling all Summer long. The introduction of Comhairle nan Eilean (The Western Isles Council) and one visit to Stornoway soon put paid to all that nonsense.

So even in a Garrynamonie without films and television we were already established in a romantic tradition; literature had seen to that. At the time I wasn't conscious of the wider romantic tradition established by music and art, but it's clear that when films and television began to make their romantic mark they were only picking up where Alasdair Alpin MacGregor, Landseer and Marjory Kennedy Fraser had left off. If song told us that the town hall clock of Stornoway chimed its message every day, then film would make sure that it kept on chiming that ridiculous message.

Above: Oscar Marzaroli *Compton Mackenzie*

For the Highlands I suppose that *Whisky Galore* may be where real life, literature and film finally coincided; the three have now become entangled in a romantic mixture of fact and fiction, history and legend, event and image. For the last forty years the real and imaginary *Whisky Galore* has been the basis from which millions have formed their impressions of the Highlands – not least the Highlanders themselves. (Incidentally, it's a remarkable fact that two Central European Jews were responsible for two of our most famous popular creations – the song *Lovely Stornoway* was written by one Mr Halpin, whilst the film script of *Whisky Galore,* an improvement on the book, was written by one Daniel Schewsky. It may be that Highland culture owes as much to the Jewish as to the Gaelic tradition. Now there's a possible thesis for students between the Bronx and Barra!)

The actual events that inspired the book and the film of *Whisky Galore* are still strong in the memories of people in South Uist, Eriskay and Barra: the sinking of *SS Politician* and the subsequent events surrounding the incident remains a reasonably common topic of conversation amongst my father's generation, and none of them say that the legend greatly distorts the reality. The truth, of course, may be that they cannot – or do not wish to – distinguish between the two any more.

Certainly the film fostered the image of the islander as a happy-go-lucky opportunist with a twinkle in his eye and a dram in his hand and that image was one that, naturally, the islanders themselves were happy to go along with. They did so, of course, with a certain sense of irony, knowing that neither they nor their creator, Compton MacKenzie, were taking themselves seriously.

There is no danger of confusion between fact and fiction when it comes to most other films about the Highlands, if only because most of these films are based upon little fact, the myths they've portrayed based upon a history that never took place and the images they've created based upon events that never happened to people who never existed. Yet these entirely foundless films are at least equally as important as the more genuine *Whisky Galore* for creating the modern visual image we have of the Highlands and the Highlander.

The most famous (or infamous) of these films is, of course, *Brigadoon*, which brought the mythic kilted Highlander living in a land of milk and heather to the attention of the whole spellbound world. If *Whisky*

Galore was important in helping to create the Highlander's image of himself, then *Brigadoon* certainly helped to create the Highlander's image for the rest of the world.

From Pennsylvania to Paris they all now knew what Scotland in general, and the Highlands in particular, was like: a place where comic tartan-wearing country folk went around singing happily of their lot in a northern Shangri La. *Brigadoon* may have done wonders for the burgeoning tartan tourist industry but, unlike *Whisky Galore,* few folk in Drinishader would have identified with it. They would, however, have identified more closely with another famous film of the post war years, *The Maggie.*

This film, based on Neil Munro's novel *Vital Spark,* was the precursor of the equally famous television series. Television programme planners now shunt the film out on wet winter afternoons in the pre-Christmas season as a filler, and it's taken on a period piece charm. The image it portrayed of the Highlander was rather in keeping with that of *Whisky Galore:* that of hapless, harmless individuals whose good nature eventually overcame their essential uselessness as they pottered about life between quayside, bar and village dance hall. (This species still survive around Lochboisdale!)

It's interesting to note that this theme of harmless eccentricity was also prominent in the most recent major film to be made about the Highlands, *Local Hero.* Here again, as in *Whisky Galore* and *The Maggie,* we had the theme of the about-to-be-exploited Highlander putting one over the potential exploiter, with local craft eventually winning over external force. But for all its good points, *Local Hero* perpetrated the myth that Highlanders, as evidenced in the character of Ben, were highly backward-looking individuals who stood in the way of progress except in so far as it might make a little bit of profit on the side for them to keep them in house or dram. This after all was the kind of behaviour that kept lovable old Dan MacPhail going forever in the *Vital Spark.* (I don't know if there was any Jewish connection in *Local Hero* but it's worth noting that in 1959 John Grierson remarked that *Whisky Galore* had been successful because of the collaboration between Highland humour and the Jewish understanding of exploitation and subjection).

Local Hero owed much of its success to two staple ingredients associated with the Highlands – beautiful scenery and self-effacing humour. One has certainly needed both in order to survive that which television has given us over the last thirty years.

Top: *The Maggie,* 1953 (B.F.I.). American title, *High and Dry*
Above: *Local Hero,* 1983 (B.F.I.)
Below: *The Highlander,* 1985 (Thorn EMI)
Below left: *Rob Roy,* 1953 (B.F.I.)

Television has, of course, become the dominant cultural force in our society and must be held largely responsible for the prevailing images of the Highlands that now exist. Ask anyone in Scotland what they think of when you mention the Highlands and the answer would most probably be either whisky or Calum Kennedy (the two are not mutually exclusive).

Television's treatment of the Highlands in the last thirty years has been dominated by two programmes – BBC's *White Heather Club* and Grampian's *Calum's Ceilidh*. Both were full of tartan and music, both were enormously successful, and both are responsible for many of the impressions that people have about the Highlands.

For years both programmes were the standard bearers for television light entertainment in Scotland. They both unquestioningly accepted, indeed were based upon, the standard (and erroneous) interpretation that Highland entertainment was about formalised dancing and strictly melodic song. The musical tradition was that of Marjory Kennedy Fraser and not that of Margaret Fay Shaw; the dancing style owed more to posh Highland balls than to remote island halls.

The *White Heather Club* and *Calum's Ceilidh* may perhaps be held particularly responsible for establishing one popular conception (or misconception) – through these programmes a close and direct association began to be formed in the public mind between the wearing of the kilt and the ability to sing a Gaelic song and play a musical instrument. It may be that the image of the singing swinging Gael was not just exemplified by Calum Kennedy – it may be that it was invented by him. (This fashionable link between the kilt and music must have worried many ordinary crofters who could rattle off a goodly song in the Claitear or play a mean accordian in the Creagorry – they must have feared that they, and their musical heritage, were now in danger of becoming worthless because they were kiltless!)

Even on Gaelic television kilts and formal song tended to dominate the day. The long running Gaelic television series *'Se Ur Beatha* projected an image of the culturally successful Highlander as someone who had won a Mod Gold Medal. Until very recently a significant part of the BBC Gaelic Department's annual budget was spent on televising the Mod, something which had not only become more and more of a cultural anachronism but which also, by virtue of its week long television coverage, reinforced the false belief that Gaelic was synonymous with the Mod.

The kind of filming that was done on these Gaelic programmes is worth a particular mention, because it established a tradition that still runs through Gaelic programmes. This is based on the presumption that because Gaelic programmes are 'unintelligible' to the passing English viewer you must stack them rich with pictures to make them tolerable. Because most of the film crews and directors were non-Gaelic these pictures were invariably, and almost exclusively, the postcard ones they presumed to be naturally Highland: peat stacks, fishing boats, the odd thatched cottage, mist about the hills and sunsets: the images that had become the standard images of the Highlands because for the last hundred years stills photographers and painters (and writers) had said that these were the important images. Television film – in Gaelic as in English programmes – reinforced these chosen images of the Highlands where landscape dominated and where, even in the 1970s, croft and creel

Above: *Reel O' Tulloch. Dancers of HM 1st Seaforth Highlanders.* Scotch Myths Archive

remained undisturbed by either Elvis Presley or the nuclear bomb.

Away from the kilt-filled realms of Light Entertainment, television's portrayal of the Highlands has been the portrayal of an eccentric place where an eccentric people with an eccentric language engage in eccentric practices (when they're not being eccentrically romantic). This view from the outside has run through nearly all television programmes about the Highlands in general, and the Western Isles in particular, whether it be humorous eccentricity as portrayed in the *Vital Spark* or religious eccentricity as portrayed in *The Last Stronghold of the Pure Gospel*. Eccentricity, of course, is the almost inevitable consequence of viewing things from the outside – wherever that outside might happen to be; in this case the broadcasting centres of power at Glasgow, Aberdeen and London. (Many things in Glasgow and London appear rather eccentric, of course, when viewed from Garrynamonie or Garrynahine – The Stock Exchange for example).

But there are notable exceptions to this general rule. In the field of drama the BBC gave us an adaptation of 7:84's *The Cheviot, The Stag, and The Black, Black Oil* – a play which took a cynical look at the new wealth promised by oil and a play which, in the passing, took a side swipe at the notion that all Highlanders spent their time at the peat fires waiting for the rain to stop.

"The Cheviot" was a much more realistic and much more political look at the Highlands than we'd been used to and, because it was transmitted nationally, must therefore have helped to clear some romantic Highland mist even in deepest Buckinghamshire. It's interesting to note that the main theme of "The Cheviot" – like that of *Whisky Galore* and *The Maggie* – was the possible exploitation of the Highlander. The treatment of that possible exploitation was, however, very different. Gone was the fey, hapless harmlessness of the Gael as portrayed in the two earlier films, and in its place was a cynicism based on an understanding of where previous promises, ranging from sheep farming to crofting tenure, had left the Highlands and the Highlander. The play used traditional music and the politically charged songs of Màiri Mhór nan Oran instead of happy choruses of *Brochan Lom*.

In recent times there have been other indications that at long last television is shaking off the Celtic twilight. In 1985 a film called *Shepherds of Berneray* was transmitted on Channel 4; an independent production by two American film makers who had spent a year on the island and gave us a portrayal of the island life of that year,

Above: *7:84 (Scotland) Theatre Company performing* The Cheviot, The Stag and The Black, Black Oil *to packed halls throughout the Highlands and Islands in 1973*

physical warts and all. The film served to remind us that life in the islands is not a bed of romantic roses, all peat cutting in the summer sun and ceilidhing in the winter evenings (though thankfully there is that). It showed that life on an isolated island is also dogged by elemental hardship, frequent torrential rain making life difficult, constant gales creating havoc and lack of secondary schools disuniting families at an early age. It also showed that Islanders can survive without the supermarket or the vet.

It's interesting to note that *Shepherds of Berneray* like an even more recent film *Hallaig* was made by independent producers. *Hallaig* – the hour-long film on the life of Sorley MacLean, has still not been shown on British television in its entirety, almost four years after it was produced. It stands however not only as a fine film and a marvellous tribute to a remarkable poet and man, but also as an artistic indictment of the prevailing philistinism of our Scottish broadcasting companies, all of whom have signally failed to produce this kind of film over the last twenty years. *Hallaig* is as much a condemnation of the mean-mindedness and the mediocrity of the Scottish public spirit as exemplified by Scottish broadcasting as it is a somewhat late but deserved eulogy for Scotland's greatest living poet.

The other more recent film which broke new territory was *Flight From Vatersay* which was shown on BBC 2's *40 Minutes* series. There was no lush, false romanticism here in the film of a lonely young man's escape from what he saw as the boredom of life on Vatersay for the excitement of life in Glasgow.

Flight From Vatersay and its subject, Neil Gillies, laid bare many of the pretences that have surrounded island life, and in particular, island exile. During the past one hundred years many youngsters have taken the path of Neil Gillies and escaped island and close family strictures to seek sexual and other freedoms elsewhere only to find that the new world was like the old, full of restrictions, failure and disappointment.

Flight From Vatersay was about disillusionment and in particular the disillusionment of the young in an island society which cannot offer them the glossy freedoms and riches that are being presented to them each night by television advertising as the norm in the late twentieth century society. Youngsters in Vatersay, like youngsters in Benbecula, and Ness, and Glasgow, and Newcastle, and Liverpool, and London, and Vancouver and New York, look around them and find ordinariness and

unemployment and alcohol and drug addiction whilst the television world suggests that others live in a world of tight jeans, fast cars and full employment. No wonder there is disillusionment, in Vatersay as much as in Handsworth.

Disillusionment, and its destructive social consequences, may be about the gap between the reality and the ideal, the gap between life as it really is and the images that are given of life as it is supposed to be. Hitherto the Highland gap was the reasonably harmless gap between the real Barra and the mythical *Brigadoon,* but now the increasingly dangerous gap is between the real disillusions of Daliburgh and the imagistic delights of *Dynasty.* If destructive social consequences are not to follow, not only do the real disillusions have to be tackled but the apparent images also have to be taken into account. Both tasks are essentially political tasks, both are urgent, and both require that the local communities should be in control, in order that life, and its images, can be relevant and fulfilling.

As the broadcasting industry stands, however, few communities have any real control over the programmes that are made and the images that are transmitted. There is little, if any, real public debate in Scotland about the philosophy of broadcasting, with the result that communities remain remote from policy, divorced from actual programming and entirely at the mercy of whatever doubtful images are given to them.

As far as the general public is concerned, television programme making, in fact, still remains an enormous mystery, something which is imbued with tremendous glamour and prestige. The general feeling is that people in Giffnock and Gearraidh Sheilidh may have a right to watch programmes, but God forbid that anybody should suggest that they have an equal right to actually make programmes about the world they live in – in other words, that they have a right to influence and control the creation of the images of the society in which they live.

Almost fifty years after the introduction of public service television broadcasting into Scotland, and twenty five years after the introduction of independent television broadcasting, the vast majority of the public remains totally ignorant about something which is actually theirs. In that long period little effort has been made at opening the doors of broadcasting knowledge to the general public, hardly any attempt has been made at educating communities in the techniques and skills of programme production, and no effort has been made at training people in how to use studios, cameras, editing facilities and all the other technology that's said to be necessary for making programmes.

The fact remains that the Highlands and the Western Isles, like all other communities, will continue to be inadequately and inaccurately portrayed as long as the Highlands and Western Isles do not have any real access to broadcasting power within their own areas. As long as they remain the passive recipients of television rather than its active participants they will be treated as peripheral and insignificant and portrayed as others see fit.

The images we have of the Highlands are the images that have been presented to us by people from outwith the area, and nowhere is that more true than in film and television. Until Highlanders themselves start making films and television programmes in sufficient quantity the long history of patronising images about the Highlands will continue. Given real access, the people of

Above: Murdo MacLeod *Archie Watching Television,* 1986

Daliburgh might even begin to create their own advertising and dramatic fantasies about young crofters in new sleek Massey Fergusons, and young fishermen who spend glossy adventurous lives fighting off Eriskay – both activities are potentially as dramatically productive and as glamorous as oil exploration off Texas.

Such film making would give people, at long last, a sense of participation in the creating of the images of the society in which they live, something which they have been denied for a long time. At the end of the day people do have a right to some form of control over the creation of these images, and that must be the philosophy by which film and television as it stands must be judged. According to that basic philosophy film and television is failing the Highlands, in much the same way that mainstream art, literature and music have failed before – by being, or becoming, the property of outsiders.

Whilst that appropriation happened there was, of course, a rich alternative culture with rich alternative images existing in the Highlands, an alternative picture that was ignored. There was another form of literature in the form of oral prose and storytelling, and there was another definition of music, in the form of folk song and traditional piping, that was overlooked for a long long time. (All this despite the tremendous efforts of people such as John Lorne Campbell, Margaret Fay Shaw, The School of Scottish Studies, The BBC's Gaelic Radio Department and so on). When it comes to the continuing appropriation of our images by film and television (even if that appropriation is by our own people), we could perhaps learn something not just from the long and sometimes comic history of our sadly misappropriated images, but also from the equally long list of possible alternative images which were forgotten or ignored.

I was in Uist recently and was reminded during that visit that the images that are now watched are not innocent slides of red hens, and the sounds that are listened to are not wavering car wireless dials picking up Luxembourg; now they watch the latest video and walk the Bornish strand with a red Sony Walkman strapped to their heads. The images and the sounds are more immediately available and are more diverse and exciting – but the images and the sounds are still not theirs. Access, participation, production and control would make them theirs.

I am reminded, finally, of an old man in Barra who, in 1970, tired of returning home to an empty house as television took over from the ceilidh, one night painted THE END in large white letters on the end of his thatched cottage. It remains an appropriate symbol for the passing of one tradition and the arrival of the brave new world. The trick may not be to try and erase the image or the words or the brave new world, but to make sure that some local people are included in the end credits that always roll after THE END, which is never really the end.

Angus Peter Campbell

Highlands and Islands: Chronology

c500	Fergus Mor crowned King of Alba at Dunadd, Argyll
563	Columba landed at Iona
843-860	Kenneth MacAlpin, King of Alba and Pictish Kingdom
c1100	Somerled, progenitor of Clan Donald and the Lordship of the Isles
1493	Forfeiture of the Lordship of the Isles
1609	The Statutes of Iona. These laws were put into effect during the reign of James VI, and were the first stage in the long process of pacifying the Highlands, and bringing the region under the control of the Scottish State
1707	Treaty of Union between Scotland and England
1715	First of two main 18th century Jacobite Risings
c1740	Beginning of the kelp industry in the West Highlands and Islands
1745	Final Jacobite Rising
1746	Battle of Culloden — the defeat of the Highland Jacobite army marked the final subjugation of clan society. The clans were disarmed, Jacobite estates forfeited, the chiefs' traditional powers withdrawn, and the wearing of Highland dress prohibited. The Highlands were finally brought under the rule of the Scottish State
1760	Introduction of large-scale sheep farming in the Highlands, and the final transition from the concept of clan lands to the private ownership of land by the clan chiefs
1773	First 'overseas' Gaelic speaking community established by Highland emigrants in Nova Scotia
1780	The Southern demand for industrial raw materials began to noticeably alter the basis of the Highland and Island economy. By the end of the century large-scale sheep farming and kelping had overtaken the rearing of black cattle as the region's main economic activity
1782	The restoration of forfeited estates
1792	Riots in Ross-shire aimed at preventing the spread of large scale sheep farming
c1800	The new economic influences accelerated the reorganisation of Highland estates. The tacksman class was eliminated and the subtenancy made into direct tenants. The old run-rig system was eradicated, instead the tenantry were allocated individual crofts — mainly along the coasts. This provided the landlords with a supply of cheap labour for kelping and fishing
1803	Passenger Vessels Act — the rearrangement of traditional social and economic structures in the Highlands had resulted in an exodus from the region of the people who had suffered as a consequence of these changes. It was the landlords' fear of the loss of their kelping labour force that persuaded the Government to pass the 1803 Act. By increasing fares it effectively halted the early emigration to America
1811-21	The Sutherland Clearances — several thousand people cleared from the interior glens to the coast
c1820	The decline of the kelp industry
1836-37	The first signs of famine
1843	The Disruption — the secession of evangelical ministers from the Established Church. In the Highlands the secession was connected with the issue of landlord patronage
1846-55	Famine and poverty throughout the Highlands and Islands
1850-55	Large scale evictions, and emigrations from the Highlands financed by government
c1850	Deer forests become a feature of the Highland landscape
1860-70s	Period of relative economic stability
1873	John Murdoch launches a new newspaper, *The Highlander,* in Inverness
1874	Bernera (Lewis) Riot. Sheriff-officers were assaulted while serving summonses of removal upon fifty-six householders in Bernera. The crofters were arrested and imprisoned. They were later put on trial and found not guilty
1881-82	The beginning of the "Crofters' War". Battle of the Braes. Skye Rent Strike. Glendale Martyrs arrested
1883	Highland Land Law Reform Association founded in London. Appointment of the Napier Commission
1884	Land agitations in Skye and Lewis. Military in Skye until early 1885
1886	Five Crofters' MPs returned to Parliament. Crofting Act becomes law (June). Creation of Crofters' Commission. Renewed agitation and further military intervention in Tiree, Skye and Pairc (Lewis)
1888	Aignish Riot (Lewis)
1891	An Comunn Gàidhealach (The Highland Association) established in Oban. An Comunn organises the National Mod and is involved in other areas of Gaelic life
1892	Deer Forest Commission
1900	Land raids in Vatersay, Lewis and other islands
1912	Board of Agriculture established
1914-18	First World War
1919	*S.S. Iolaire* disaster. Coll and Gress farms raided
1920	Land raids in North Uist, Skye, Raasay, Sutherland and elsewhere
1923	Stornoway Trust set up to administer Parish of Stornoway for its inhabitants
1939-45	Second World War
1948	Knoydart Land Raids
1951	Foundation of School of Scottish Studies at Edinburgh University
1954	Taylor Commission Report on Crofting areas
1955	Crofting (Scotland) Act
1965	Highlands and Islands Development Board established in Inverness
1968	Gaelic Books Council established
1972	*The West Highland Free Press* founded in Skye
1973	The Crofting Reform Bill. *The Cheviot, The Stag and The Black, Black Oil* tour: 7:84 (Scotland) Theatre Company
1975	Foundation of Comhairle nan Eilean, the Western Isles Islands Council, following the re-organisation of local government
1976	Arnish (Lewis) Oil Platform Yard
1977	Acair set up as a bilingual publishing company in the Western Isles
1979	Radio nan Eilean, the Gaelic radio station for the Islands, goes on the air
1981	Planning permission given for a NATO base in Stornoway — in spite of the high degree of local opposition
1983	Sabhal Mor Ostaig, the Gaelic College in Skye, begins the only Gaelic further education course (in Business Management and Related Studies) in existence at present
1984	Museum nan Eilean opens
1985	New Crofters Union formed. CNAG — new Gaelic pressure group
1985	An Lanntair Art Gallery opens in Stornoway
1986	Salmon Bill going through Parliament. Although some of its considerable powers have been modified it is still regarded as another example of legislation to benefit Highland landlords. *As an Fhearann* the exhibition opens, and *As an Fhearann* the book is published

Compiled by Joni Buchanan

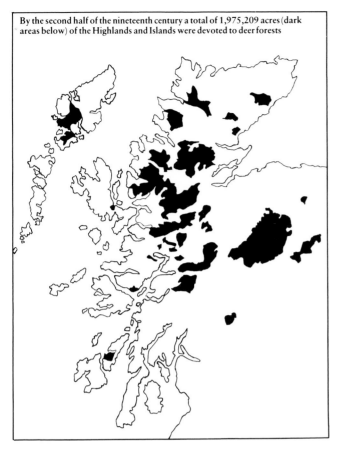

By the second half of the nineteenth century a total of 1,975,209 acres (dark areas below) of the Highlands and Islands were devoted to deer forests

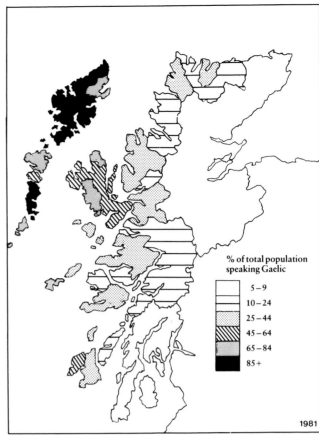

% of total population speaking Gaelic

	5 – 9
	10 – 24
	25 – 44
	45 – 64
	65 – 84
	85 +

1981

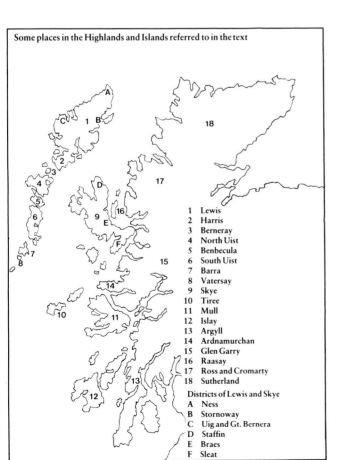

Some places in the Highlands and Islands referred to in the text

1 Lewis
2 Harris
3 Berneray
4 North Uist
5 Benbecula
6 South Uist
7 Barra
8 Vatersay
9 Skye
10 Tiree
11 Mull
12 Islay
13 Argyll
14 Ardnamurchan
15 Glen Garry
16 Raasay
17 Ross and Cromarty
18 Sutherland

Districts of Lewis and Skye
A Ness
B Stornoway
C Uig and Gt. Bernera
D Staffin
E Braes
F Sleat

Statistics for the Highlands and Islands

Population (Based on Census Figures)

1921	371,372
1951	316,471
1961	307,532
1981	353,513

Between 1850 and 1950 the population of the Highlands is estimated to have fallen by 100,000.

Unemployment (Based on Manpower Services Commission Figures)

1984		
	Female Unemployment	11.2%
	Male Unemployment	16.2%
	Total Average	14.2%

These statistics are for the whole of what may be called the Highlands and Islands. The final total is superficially low, however, bearing in mind that male unemployment figures in 1984 for the Western Isles, Skye & Wester Ross, Sutherland and Campbeltown were, respectively, 25.5%, 26.1%, 31.9% and 21.2%. These compare against Thurso with 9.8%, Orkney at 13.1% and Shetland at 6.4%, areas benefiting from oil development and exploration.

Gaelic Speakers 1981 (Based on CNAG Figures)

Highland Region (Pop. 187,004)	Number who either speak, read or write Gaelic
Male	8,004
Female	9,094
Total	17,098
Percentage of total population	9.6%
Western Isles (Pop. 30,713)	Number who either speak, read or write Gaelic
Male	11,557
Female	12,032
Total	23,589
Percentage of total population	80.0%

Crofts

According to figures supplied by the Crofters' Commission, Inverness, there were 17,734 registered crofts in the Highlands and Islands at the end of April 1986.

105

Highlands and Islands:
A Selected Bibliography

Political, Economic and Social History

R.J. Adam (ed): *Papers on Sutherland Estate Management 1802-1816;* Scottish History Society (2 Vols), Edinburgh 1972 : *John Hume's Survey of Assynt;* Scottish History Society, Edinburgh 1960

J.S. Blackie: *Altvona,* Edinburgh 1882 : *The Scottish Highlander and the Land Laws,* London 1885

T. Brown: *Annals of the Disruption,* Edinburgh 1890

J. Bryden and G. Houston: *Agrarian Change in the Scottish Highlands,* London 1976

J.M. Bumsted: *The People's Clearance: Highland Emigration to British North America,* Edinburgh and Manitoba 1982

E. Burt: *Letters from a Gentleman in the North of Scotland,* London 1815

A.D. Cameron: *Go Listen to the Crofters,* Stornoway 1986

G.D. Campbell (Duke of Argyll): 'A Corrected Picture of the Highlands'; *Nineteenth Century* (Vol 16), 1884

G. Carter: 'The Changing Image of the Scottish Peasantry 1745-1980' in R. Samuel's (ed) *People's History and Socialist Theory,* London 1981

G.B. Clark: *The Highland Land Question,* London 1885

S. Clark: *Social Origins of the Irish Land War,* Princeton 1979

D. Cooper: *Skye,* London 1970

H.L. Cowan: *British Emigration to North America,* Toronto 1961

E.R. Cregeen (ed): *The Argyll Estate Instructions 1771-1805;* Scottish History Society, Edinburgh 1964 : 'The Tacksmen and their Successors' in *Scottish Studies* (Vol 13), Edinburgh 1969

L.M. Cullen: *An Economic History of Ireland since 1660,* London 1972

F. Fraser Darling: *West Highland Survey,* Oxford 1955

J.P. Day: *Public Administration in the Highlands and Islands of Scotland,* London 1918

T.M. Devine: 'Highland Migration to Lowland Scotland 1760-1860'; *Scottish Historical Review* (Vol 62), 1983 : 'Temporary Migration and the Scottish Highlands in the Nineteenth Century'; *Economic History Review* (Vol 32), 1979

P. Gaskell: *Morven Transformed,* Cambridge 1968

I.F. Grant: *The MacLeods: The History of a Clan,* London 1959

J. Grassie: *Highland Experiment,* Aberdeen 1983

M. Gray: *The Highland Economy 1750-1850,* Edinburgh 1957 : 'The Highland Potato Famine of the 1840s'; *Economic History Review* (Vol 7), 1954-5 : 'The Kelp Industry in the Highlands and Islands of Scotland'; *Economic History Review* (Vol 4), 1951 : *The Fishing Industries of Scotland 1790-1914,* Aberdeen 1978

W.R. Greg: 'Highland Destitution and Irish Emigration'; *Quarterly Review* (Vol 90), 1851

I. Grimble: *Highland Man,* Inverness 1980 : 'Emigration in the Time of Rob Donn 1714-1778'; *Scottish Studies* (Vol 7), Edinburgh 1963 : *The Trial of Patrick Sellar,* London 1962

I. Fraser Grigor: *Mightier than a Lord,* Stornoway 1979

J. Hunter: 'The Emergence of the Crofting Community: the Religious Contribution 1798-1843'; *Scottish Studies* (Vol 18), 1974 : *The Making of the Crofting Community,* Edinburgh 1976 : 'Sheep and Deer: Highland Sheep Farming 1850-1900'; *Northern Scotland* (Vol 1), 1973 : *For the People's Cause: From the Writings of John Murdoch,* HMSO 1986

J. Lee: 'The Ribbon Men' in T.D. Williams' (ed) *Secret Societies in Ireland,* Dublin 1973

R.D. Lobban: *The Migration of Highlanders to Lowland Scotland 1750-1890;* PH.D. Thesis, University of Edinburgh 1969

J. Loch: *An Account of the Improvements on the Estates of the Marquess of Stafford,* London 1820

K.J. Logue: *Popular Disturbances in Scotland 1780-1815,* Edinburgh 1977

D.J. MacCuish: 'The Origin and Development of Crofting Law'; *Transactions of the Gaelic Society of Inverness* (Vol 43), 1962

C.S. MacDonald: *Early Highland Emigration to Nova Scotia and Prince Edward Island 1770-1853;* Nova Scotia Historical Society Collections (Vol 23), 1941

D. MacDonald: *Lewis, A History of the Island,* Edinburgh 1978

J. McEwen: *Who Owns Scotland,* Edinburgh 1981

J. McGrath: *The Cheviot, The Stag and The Black, Black Oil,* Kyleakin 1974

J. MacInnes: *The Evangelical Movement in the Highlands of Scotland 1688-1800,* Aberdeen 1951

M. MacKay: 'Nineteenth Century Tiree Emigrant Communities in Ontario'; *Oral History Journal* (Vol 9), 1981

A. MacKenzie: *The Highland Clearances,* Inverness 1883 : *The Isle of Skye 1882-1883,* Inverness 1883

D. MacLeod: *The Sutherland Clearances,* Glasgow 1856 : *Gloomy Memories,* Glasgow 1892

K. Marx: 'Sutherland and Slavery, or the Duchess at Home'; *The People's Paper,* March 15th 1853

D. Meyer: *The Highland Scots of North Carolina 1732-1776,* London 1961

H. Millar: *Sutherland as it was, and is, or How a Country may be Ruined,* Edinburgh 1843

R. Mitchison: 'The Highland Clearances'; *Scottish Economic and Social History* (Vol 1), 1981

I.R.M. Mowat: *Easter Ross 1750-1850,* Edinburgh 1980

N. Murray: *The Scottish Handloom Weavers 1790-1850,* Edinburgh 1978

W. Orr: *Deer Forests, Landlords and Crofters,* Edinburgh 1982

J. Prebble: *Culloden,* London 1961 : *The Highland Clearances,* London 1963 : *Glencoe,* London 1966

E. Richards: *The Leviathan of Wealth,* London 1973 : *A History of the Highland Clearances: Agrarian Transformation and the Evictions 1746-1886* (Vol 1), London 1982: *Emigration, Protest, Reasons* (Vol 2), London 1985

D. Ross: *The Glengarry Evictions,* Glasgow 1853 : *Real Scottish Grievances,* Glasgow 1854

T.C. Smout: *A History of the Scottish People 1560-1830,* London 1969

D. Stewart: *Sketches of the Character, Manners, and Present State of the Highlanders of Scotland,* Edinburgh 1822

F. Thompson: *The Highlands and Islands,* London 1974

J. Walker: *An Economical History of the Hebrides and Highlands of Scotland,* Edinburgh 1812

A.J. Youngson: *After the Forty Five,* Edinburgh 1973

Poetry and Prose

A.J. Aitken, M.P. McDiarmid, D.S. Thomson (eds): *Bards and Makars,* Glasgow 1977

O. Andersson: 'On Gaelic Folk Music from the Isle of Lewis' in *Budklaven,* Abo 1952

E. Bassin: *The Old Songs of Skye: Frances Tolmie and her circle,* London 1977

J.S. Blackie: *The Language and Literature of the Scottish Highlands,* Edinburgh 1876

H. Blair: *A Critical Dissertation on the Poems of Ossian,* London 1763

A. Caimbeul: *Moll is Cruithneachd,* Glasgow 1972 : *Suathadh ri Iomadh Rubha,* Glaschu 1973

A. Caimbeul: *Bardachd a' Bhocsair,* Loanhead 1978

I. Caimbeul: *Poems,* Edinburgh 1884

T. Caimbeul: *Deireadh an Fhoghair,* Dun Eideann 1979

G. Calder: *The Gaelic Songs of Duncan MacIntyre,* Edinburgh 1912

J.F. Campbell: *Leabhar na Feinne,* London 1872 : *Popular Tales of the West Highlands,* Paisley 1890-93

J.L. Campbell: *Gaelic Folksongs from the Isle of Barra,* London 1950 : *Highland Songs of the Forty-Five,* Edinburgh 1933 : *Fr Allan McDonald of Eriskay 1859-1905, Priest, Poet and Folklorist,* Edinburgh 1954

J.L. Campbell and F. Collinson: *Hebridean Folksongs* (3 Vols), Oxford 1969-81

H. Creighton, C.I. MacLeod: *Gaelic Songs in Nova Scotia,* Ottawa 1964

D. Domhnallach: *Domhnall Ruadh Choruna*, Glasgow 1969

T. Domhnallach: *Creach Mhor nam Fiadh*, Stornoway 1973

E. Gillies: *Sean Dain agus Orain Ghaidhealach*, Perth 1786

N. Gunn: *The Silver Darlings*, London 1941 : *Butcher's Broom*, Edinburgh 1934

D. Caimbeul Hay: *Fuaran Sleibh*, Glasgow 1947

D.E. Meek: *Màiri Mhór nan Oran*,Glasgow 1977

D. MacAmhlaigh: *Seobhrach as a' Chlaich*, Glasgow 1967 : (ed) *Nua-bhardachd Ghaidhlig/Modern Scottish Gaelic Poems*, Edinburgh 1976

F. MacColla: *The Albannach*, London 1932 : *And the Cock Crew*, Glasgow 1945

Coinneach D. MacDhòmhnaill (ed): *Briseadh na Cloiche agus sgeulachdan eile*, Glasgow 1970

R. MacDonald: *Leth-cheud Bliadhna (Contemporary Poems in Gaelic and English)*, Glasgow 1978

M. MacDhòmhnaill: *The Emigrant Experience*, Toronto 1982

C. MacFhearghuis: *Suileabhan*, Glaschu 1983

S. MacGill-Eain (Sorley MacLean): *Reothairt is Contraigh/Spring tide and Neap tide*, Edinburgh 1977 : *Ris a' Bhruthaich: The Criticism and Prose Writings of Sorley MacLean*, Stornoway 1985

S. MacGill-Eain and R. Garioch: *17 Poems for 6d*, Edinburgh 1939

D.I. MacIomhair (ed): *Eadar Peann is Paipear*, Glasgow 1985

D. MacLean: 'The Literature of the Scottish Gael' in *Celtic Review 7*, Edinburgh 1912

G.R.D. MacLean: *Poems of the Western Highlands*, London 1961

S. MacLean: *The Poetry of the Clearances*; Transactions of the Gaelic Society of Inverness (Vol 38), 1962

I.N. MacLeoid: *Bardachd Leodhais*, Glasgow 1916

F. MacLeoid: *Na Balaich air Ronaidh*, Aberdeen 1972

A. MacNeacail: *An Cathadh mor – The Great Snow Battle*, (Illus. by Simon Fraser), Nairn 1984

M. MacPharlain: *An Toinneamh Diomhair*, Stornoway 1973

M. MacPherson: *Gaelic Poems and Songs*, Inverness 1891

R. MacThomais: *An Dealbh Briste*, Edinburgh 1951 : *Creachadh na Clarsaich* Edinburgh 1982

W. Matheson: *The Blind Harper: An Clarsair Dall*, Edinburgh 1970

D. Meek: *Màiri Mhor nan Oran*, Glasgow 1977 : 'Gaelic Poets of the Land Agitation'; Transactions of the Gaelic Society of Inverness (Vol 49), Inverness 1977

I. Moireach: *An Aghaidh Choimheach*, Glasgow 1973

D.M. Morison, J.A. MacKenzie, J. MacLeod (eds): *Eilean Fraoich: Lewis Gaelic Songs and Melodies*, Stornoway 1982

I.C. Smith: *Consider the Lilies*, London 1968 : *Selected Poems 1955-1980*, Edinburgh 1981 : *The Exiles*, Manchester 1984

D.S. Thomson: *An Introduction to Gaelic Poetry*, London 1974

M.F. Shaw: *Folksongs and Folklore of South Uist*, London 1955

I. Stephen: *Malin, Hebrides, Minches*, Denmark 1983 (Poems by I. Stephen, photographs by S. Maynard)

Photography

M. Buchanan: *St. Kilda: A Photographic Album*, Edinburgh 1983

D. Cooper: *Skye Remembered*, Skye 1984

D. MacAulay: *George Washington Wilson in the Hebrides*, Aberdeen 1983

A. MacDonald, S. MacLeod (eds): *A Lewis Album*, Stornoway 1982

C. Maclean, J. Hunter: *Skye the Island*, Edinburgh 1986

O. Marzaroli: *One Man's World: Photographs 1955-84*, Glasgow 1984

L.M.H. Smith: *The Road to the Isles – The Hebrides in Lantern Slides*, Loanhead 1983

P. Strand: *Tir a' Mhurain*, London 1962

F. Thompson: *Victorian and Edwardian Highlands From Old Photographs*, London 1976

G. Wylie: *Patterns of the Hebrides (Gaelic – Cur is Dluth)*, London 1981

G. Wylie: *The Hebrides*, Glasgow 1978

Above: Alexander Moffat *Iain Crichton Smith*. Oil on canvas, 36″ × 36″, 1980. Collection of the Scottish Arts Council

General

R. Ayton: *A Voyage Round Great Britain*, with views drawn by W. Daneill, 8 Vols, London 1814-25

D. Beaton: *Bibliography of Gaelic Books, Pamphlets and Magazine Articles of Caithness and Sutherland*, Wick 1925

A. Bruford: 'Recitation or Re-creation – examples of South Uist Storytelling'; *Scottish Studies (Vol 22)*, Edinburgh 1978

J.B. Caird: 'Changes in the Highlands and Islands of Scotland 1951-1971'; *Geoforum 12*, 1972

J. Cameron: *The Old and New Highlands and Hebrides*, Kirkcaldy 1972

D. Campbell and R.A. MacLean: *Beyond the Atlantic Roar: A Study of the Nova Scotia Scots*, Toronto 1974

M. Chapman: *The Gaelic Vision in Scottish Culture*, London 1978

J. MacMaster Campbell: *An Comunn Gaidhealach, its Accomplishments and Aspirations*, Glasgow 1927

R.W. Chapman (ed): *Johnson and Boswell: A Journey to the Western Islands of Scotland; A Journal of a Tour to the Hebrides (1773)*, London 1924

D. Cooper: *Road to the Isles — Travellers in the Hebrides, 1770-1914*, London 1979

M. Ferguson and A. Matheson: *Scottish Gaelic Union Catalogue*, Edinburgh 1984

Gaelic Books Council: *Leabhraichean Gaidhlig: A Classified Catalogue of Gaelic and Gaelic-related Books in Print*, Glasgow 1983

D.J. MacLeod: *Twentieth Century Publications in Scottish Gaelic*, Edinburgh 1980

J. Murray and C. Morrison: *Bilingual Primary Education in the Western Isles, Scotland*, Stornoway 1984

Stewart and Thompson: *Scotland's Forged Tartans*, Edinburgh 1980

M.C. Storrie: 'Islay, a Hebridean Exception'; *Geographical Review 57*, 1961

D.S. Thomson: *The Companion to Gaelic Scotland*, Oxford 1983

F. Thompson: *The Uists and Barra*, Newton Abbot 1974

Recorded Music: Gaelic

A selection of songs, music and stories is available in the series *Scottish Tradition* produced by Tangent Records for the University of Edinburgh. The recordings are from the tape archives of the School of Scottish Studies and further information about the series is available from the School of Scottish Studies, Edinburgh University, 27 George Square, Edinburgh EH8 9LD or from Topic Records, 50 Stroud Green Road, London NE4 3EF.

Lismor Recordings produce a wide selection of records of Scottish Dance Music, piping and popular Gaelic and Scottish songs. Their address is 42 Kilmarnock Road, Glasgow G41.

Another label which in recent years has produced a number of excellent records featuring some of the most popular traditional Gaelic singers is Temple Records. Information about their recordings is available from Robin Morton, Temple Record Studios, Shillinghill, Temple, Midlothian.

The rock group *Run Rig* have created a successful fusion of rock music and the Gaelic musical tradition. They have recorded several excellent albums and cassettes.

Contributors' Biographical Notes

Angus Peter Campbell was born and brought up, until the age of twelve, on the island of South Uist. His family then moved to Clachan on the Isle of Seil near Oban. He went to school at Garrynamonie Primary in South Uist and to Oban High School. He is an honours graduate in Politics and Modern History from Edinburgh University.

Since leaving University he has worked as a journalist with The West Highland Free Press, BBC Radio Highland and Grampian Television. He now works as a freelance writer, contributing a weekly column on broadcasting to The West Highland Free Press.

He also writes poetry, and took part in last year's tour of Ireland by Scottish artists and musicians. He lives in Inverness-shire.

John McGrath was born in Liverpool in 1938, and educated at Liverpool and Oxford. His earlier writing includes *Events While Guarding the Bofors Gun*, and the original *Z Cars* television series.

He is also founder and director of 7:84 Theatre Company, which produced the now legendary *The Cheviot, The Stag and The Black, Black Oil* in 1973. Since 1973, 7:84's work has endorsed and celebrated its close association with the struggles and achievements of the Highlands and Islands, in such notable productions as *Blood Red Roses*, 1981; *The Catch (Red Herrings in the Minch)*, 1982; and *There is a Happy Land*, 1986.

Sorley MacLean was born and raised in the township of Osgaig, Isle of Raasay. He graduated from Edinburgh University in 1933; was schoolmaster in Edinburgh and later Plockton, Ross-shire and is now retired from teaching and living in the Braes district of Skye, where his great-grandmother's people once lived. He has received Honorary degrees from three Universities. Through his poetry he has inspired in large measure the considerable flowering of creative writing in Gaelic since the war.

Finlay MacLeod lives in Shawbost in Lewis, with his wife Norma and two young daughters Ceit Anna and Raonailt. He was born in Ness in 1937. Like many Lewismen, he has had numerous forms of employment and been to University. Since returning home some years ago he has been involved in education — especially in Gaelic education – and publishing. He has written extensively in Gaelic, particularly children's books and plays for radio. He has a strong interest in the Hebrides, Humanism and hill-walking. He has also had an intimate and ambivalent relationship with crofting since he was a child.

Alexander Moffat was born in Dunfermline in 1943. He was Director of the New 57 Gallery in Edinburgh from 1969 to 1977 and since 1979 has taught painting at Glasgow School of Art. In 1973 he had a one-man exhibition *A view of the portrait* at the Scottish National Portrait Gallery and in 1978 he was commissioned by the Scottish Arts Council to paint portraits of seven of the most prominent 20th century Scottish poets. The resulting exhibition *Seven Poets* was toured throughout the United Kingdom by Third Eye Centre from 1981 to 1983. He has recently co-selected the second *British Art Show* (1984) for the Arts Council of Great Britain and selected *New Image: Glasgow* (1985) for Third Eye Centre. Alexander Moffat has works in many major collections including the Pushkin Museum in Moscow and the Yale Center for British Art, New Haven, Connecticut.

John Murray has been involved at the forefront of many recent initiatives in the arts, publishing, broadcasting education and rural community development.

As a Gaelic writer he is best known for his short stories, stage plays and children's books. He has also published professional work in English.

A BAD SEASON

Sportsman. "I can assure you, what with the rent of the moor, and my expenses, and 'what not,' the birds have cost me—ah—a sovereign apiece!!"
Keeper. "A' weel, sir! 'Deed it's a maircy ye didna kill na mair o' 'em!!"

Above: *Punch* Magazine

Above: Donald Morrison *Returning home with the cows in the evening*, 1930s

Below: *Original 7:84 poster for "The Cheviot . . . "*, 1973